If It Were Just Dad

Robert Jones

If It Were Just Dad

Published in the United States of America.

Cover Art: Diane Jones

Author Photo Credit: Chenaille Photo & Video – Chenaillephoto.com

ISBN: 978-1-7353972-4-5 paperback

978-1-7353972-5-2 eBook

If It Were Just Dad

Finding Hope
in the Midst of a Tempest

Robert Jones

First and foremost, this book is dedicated to my Lord and Savior, Jesus Christ. I owe everything to You. Apart from You I can do nothing. There is no story without You. May You be glorified through it.

This story is a tribute to my hero, Robert W. Jones. You fought the good fight and finished well.

It is also a tribute to my mother, Shirley Jones, who taught me so much. Praying you experience the healing, peace, joy and abundant blessings that only come from the Lord, Jesus Christ.

To both Dad and Mom: Thank you for raising and loving me.

To my wife and best friend, Diane: Words cannot express how grateful I am for your love, support, and compassion. You have treated my parents like your own and I could not have survived this storm without you. God gave me an indescribable gift when He gave me you. I love you.

To Joanna, my writing coach, editor, and sister-in-Christ: Thank you for your patience, expertise, Godly wisdom, and friendship.

To Bill and Carolyn Chenaille, Christian friends and expert photographers: Thank you for your kindness and generosity.

Contents

Note from a Nobody

In the Introduction to my first book, *Average Man, Almighty Companion*, I wrote this:

> *I'm an average guy; a "nobody" to most people. I am really just a face in the crowd. I am not a pastor, a Bible scholar, nor a counselor. I am a recovering pessimist, skeptic, and cynic. I've struggled with feelings of inadequacy, pride, anxiety, uncertainty, regret, guilt, and loss. I've worried about my marriage, children, career, finances, the state of our world, and what others think of me. I can put on a good front, and a happy face, but sometimes unseen battles rage in my mind. From my perspective, I have no tangible qualifications to be an author.*

I wrote the foregoing words back in 2020 and they are as true today as they were then. I never dreamed that I'd ever publish one book, let alone two, but here I am with number three. It is only by God's grace, strength, and wisdom that this is possible. I cling to John 15:5 where Jesus says, "I am the vine; you are the branches. If you remain in Me and I in you, you will bear much fruit; apart from Me you can do nothing." Indeed, apart from Him there is nothing good in me.

More than forty years ago I was a young college student, ambitious, and full of pride. I wanted nothing to do with God and considered myself a card-carrying skeptic. I questioned everything and pursued many avenues in search of meaning and "happiness." Both continually eluded me.

I avoided facing the reality that this life is very short and none of us is guaranteed tomorrow. James 4:14 is just one of many Bible verses which convey this truth: "Why, you do not even know what will happen tomorrow. What is your life? You are a mist that appears for a little while and then vanishes." Deep down, even as someone who was not a devoted follower of Jesus Christ, I knew the truth of this verse but didn't embrace it. I lived like I had time to figure things out and "get right" with God. I was so wrong.

Related to the foregoing truth, I didn't think about one of the basic questions of life: What happens when I die? I thought I had time to face the question of my own mortality. I believed that God graded on a curve, and I'd get my act together—someday. Well into my late twenties I put my faith in my career, making money, recognition, family, and countless other things. There is nothing inherently wrong with the foregoing pursuits, but they were the objects of my faith and affection, what the Bible would call "idols." Eventually I would come to the realization that any or all of those things could vanish in an instant.

The fact is, my sin separated me from God and I was actually what the Bible calls an "enemy of the Cross" (Philippians 3:18). I am eternally grateful that He brought me to a place where I recognized my sinfulness, brokenness, and hopelessness. I needed a Savior, someone to forgive my sins and change the direction of my life. Thank God that Jesus paid my sin debt in full when He shed His blood on the Cross, for my sin and yours. He loved me even when I had rejected Him. Accepting His payment for sin is the only way to be right with God and to find true meaning in this life. And that changed everything for me. 2 Corinthians 5:17, one of my favorite verses, says this: "Therefore, if anyone is in Christ, the new creation has come: The old has gone, the new is here!" I can't add anything to that.

Knowing Jesus Christ as my personal Savior is the greatest joy in my life. I can't imagine living apart from Him. But the Bible also tells us that life is difficult, whether you're a Christian or an unbeliever. Which leads me to the reason I wrote this book.

This "storm," as I'll refer to it, has tested my faith and brought me face-to-face again with the hard questions and brevity of life. And it has not been pretty. Being transparent, I haven't always passed the test. I am not the sharpest tool in the shed and sometimes it takes me a while. Thank God that He is patient with me. It is only due to His presence in my life that I am still standing. The reason I prayerfully decided to go ahead with publication is not due to the incredible events of this storm. It's how God has carried me every moment. It is a story of hope, and I want Him to be glorified through it. It is not about me.

So here goes once again. This is probably my last book unless the Lord has something else for me to share.

God bless you and keep your eyes fixed on our Lord and Savior, Jesus Christ!

Your friend,

Bob

Lessons From the Storm

If you declare with your mouth, "Jesus is Lord," and believe in your heart that God raised Him from the dead, you will be saved.

Romans 10:9

S torms. What comes to mind when you hear that word? For me, I think about extreme weather disturbances such as hurricanes, tornados, floods, fires, and other natural disasters. Sadly, these events seem to be prevalent in our world today. Close to home I recall severe storms of the past when blizzards and heavy rain resulted in real damage to lives and property.

Storms can cause pain and loss. Some pass quickly, leaving little if any damage behind. Other storms are vicious. Sometimes it is difficult, if not impossible, to fully recover. I think it's safe to say that most of us can probably relate to at least one storm in our personal lives.

The word "storm" is a strong metaphor for trials, the difficult things we go through in this life. Jesus told a story in Matthew 7:24-26 which tells of such a storm. I love the parables in the Bible and can especially relate to this one:

Therefore everyone who hears these words of Mine and puts them into practice is like a wise man who built his house on the rock. The rain came down, the streams rose, and the winds blew and beat against that house; yet it did not fall, because it had its foundation on the rock. But everyone who hears these words of Mine and does not put them into practice is like a foolish man who built his house on sand. The rain came down, the streams rose, and the winds blew and beat against that house, and it fell with a great crash.

There are a number of truths one can learn from this story but one stands out to me: the fact that the rain and the wind beat against the homes of both the wise and foolish builders. Storms are no respecters of persons. But the real, practical lesson for me hinges on this question: What is my foundation built on? Or more appropriately, on whom is my foundation built? Is it Jesus Christ or someone else? Is it God's Word, the Holy Bible, or something else? When storms or trials of life hit, is my foundation strong enough to leave me standing? Is yours? In this parable, only one house is left standing. The one with the foundation built on Him and obedience to His word.

I'm reminded of my late grandfather, Pop's, favorite hymn: "On Christ the Solid Rock," written in 1834 by Edward Mote. The words to this hymn parallel the big idea in Matthew 7: "On Christ the Solid Rock I stand, all other ground is sinking sand…"

I need to lean daily on verses like Colossians 3:2 which tell me to "Set my mind on things above, not on earthly things" (my paraphrase). And verse 3 reminds me of who I truly am: "For you died, and your life is now hidden with Christ in God." My heart's desire is to rely totally on Jesus Christ, my firm foundation.

Many books have been written about trials and suffering in the life of the believer. Trials (storms) and hardships are nothing new. In fact, Jesus makes it clear in John 16:33 that they are to be expected in this life. And 1 Peter 4:12 tells us, "Dear friends, do not be surprised at the fiery ordeal that has come on you to test you, as though something strange were happening to you." I trust God's Word completely and understand that, while storms are a reality, God is in control and will be there for us. But storms are also personal and each of us deal with things in our own way. What might not be a big deal for me may be devastating for someone else. How could I possibly know what you might be going through?

Most people probably do not relish going through difficult times. I certainly don't. But the storm has taught me a number of lessons which you'll see throughout this book.

Above all, it has drawn me into a deeper relationship with the Lord and increased my desire for His Word. For that I am grateful, and, with His help and strength, I'll keep pressing on, one day at a time.

If you read my first book, *Average Man*, you know that I've been journaling in my quiet time since the 1990s. Since this story is based on my journal entries, it tends to be chronological. It also reflects the emotions and feelings I had at the time I recorded the events. I am human and vulnerable, and there were times when I could not see a way out. That said, despite the intensity of the storm and my often-imperfect response to it, God's goodness, love, grace and mercy are written all over this story. So, I pray that you read it until the end and take encouragement from it. Above all, let me make it absolutely clear that my purpose is to give God the glory, for all He has done throughout my life and in this storm.

When I was at rock bottom and things seemed hopeless, I was faced with this question: "Do I trust His Word or don't I?" While I don't understand why things happened the way they did, the answer is a resounding "yes" for me. He has never let go of me and loves me in spite of who I am. My sincere prayer is that you will find hope in the midst of whatever storm you may be going through. There are lessons to be learned and blessings to be received …

May the God of hope fill you with all joy and peace as you trust in Him, so that you may overflow with hope by the power of the Holy Spirit.

Romans 15:13

Lessons from Running

Therefore, since we are surrounded by such a great cloud of witnesses, let us throw off everything that hinders and the sin that so easily entangles. And let us run with perseverance the race marked out for us, fixing our eyes on Jesus, the pioneer and perfecter of faith. For the joy set before Him He endured the cross, scorning its shame, and sat down at the right hand of the throne of God. Consider Him who endured such opposition from sinners, so that you will not grow weary and lose heart.

Hebrews 12:1-3

Just past the turnaround, only a mile-and-a-half to go, and I'm starting to gasp for breath. Besides that, my legs are burning and there are still two hills to navigate before the stretch to the finish line. The wind is blowing, and the temperature is around thirty-degrees Fahrenheit. Why did I decide to run this race this morning? It would have been easier to stay in bed where it's warm.

I am not a runner. Almost in my mid-sixties, I started training back in April of 2024. I made a promise to my middle daughter that I would join her on Thanksgiving morning in the annual "Turkey Trot" 5K race. After years of watching my three girls' many races and observing the camaraderie of the running community, I wanted to share in that experience.

This past summer I decided to run in a local one-mile race where I met my simple goal of finishing and remaining upright. A few months later, on a whim, I ran in my first 5K race ever! I wanted to see if my training had prepared me for this type of race. It was hard, and I had to stop and walk a few times, but I finished with a time that was not terrible. It felt good and was rewarding to finish the race.

After a setback in September with back pain and some effective chiropractic treatment, I kept my promise and ran the Turkey Trot with my middle daughter. This race was the whole reason I started training back in April. I was blessed to run with both my middle and oldest daughters. I ran (no walking) the entire race and shaved almost five minutes off of my best time! It was a wonderful experience, and I was content. I had no plans to run any more races this year.

But here I was, a week later, running in this Christmas 5K. It was probably a mistake to sign up in the first place.

Besides the fact that it's windy and freezing cold, I had not trained adequately for the past week. Right after the Turkey Trot, I was sick for a couple days and didn't run at all. And now I learned that my middle daughter, who was going to run this race with me, is under the weather so she's a no-show. She was the main reason I signed up! After some debating in my mind, and prayer (what I should have done first), I made the decision to participate this morning.

With about a mile to go I prayed that God would give me the strength to keep going, to not give up. I lifted my eyes and then noticed a female runner just ahead of me. I hadn't noticed her before and thought, *where did she come from?* I reasoned that I'd be okay if I could keep up with her because she was running at about my speed. I caught up with the young lady and told her that she was my "mark," and I was trying to stay at a pace just behind her. We ran in tandem and then, in addition to my legs burning and trying to catch my breath, my side began to hurt. My newfound partner told me to stretch my right arm up, over my head. I was incredulous but that motion did reduce the pain in my side. She said, "Running is hard but you're doing great. I've been running for ten years and you've kept up with me." That remark was encouraging!

When I felt that I couldn't make it up the final hill without stopping, my new friend said, "You can do this, don't give up, you're almost there, you'll overtake me at the finish..." She followed up with, "I know it's hard but you're going to feel great when it's over."

It's amazing how the right words at the right time can make a difference. I wanted to stop and walk so badly but I kept going as she said, "Just one more hill, don't stop, you can do this..." I felt a supernatural boost of strength into the final stretch. As we came towards the finish I said, "You go ahead and finish before me, I couldn't have done this without you." She thanked me and crossed the finish line about a second before I did. She gave me a high-five at the end and said, "Well-done." I may never see this woman again, but I was able to finish, in large part, because of her encouragement. I have no doubt that she was the answer to the prayer I prayed when I felt like giving up.

To me, running is a metaphor for this journey we call "life." Things can be going okay and then we hit a difficult hill, and we experience pain. Similar to my experience in this race, we can be unprepared for the challenge. Sometimes we don't know how we will continue and it seems easiest just to give up. You can start out well and then falter at the end. Or maybe like me in my own life, you can start poorly and hopefully finish well. At least that is my goal.

Now I know that any serious runner who reads this will be thinking, "Bob, you're a piker. It's just a 3.1-mile race! Marathons, trail races, and fifty-milers are much more difficult." I agree; I'll probably never run more than a 5K. But

I still think that this fits the metaphor. The trial, or "storm" as I'll refer to it, pales in comparison to "races" others are running. But they are still trials, nonetheless.

Caring for my parents over the past number of years has been a lot like running a difficult race. There have been times during the race when it's been "downhill," where I've felt confident and good about things. And then there have been those challenging "hills" where I've wanted to stop and give up. But the fact is, God has continually brought people into my life who have in essence said, "You're doing great, keep going, you're almost there." Without that encouragement from the Lord and the people He continues to bring across my path, I would have stumbled and fallen. And He continues to orchestrate these divine moments which keep me going.

In my life I have found that it's comfortable to take the easy way out when it comes to doing "hard" things. Deciding to be a no-show for the Christmas race would have been the easiest thing to do that morning. And there have been many times in the past where I've taken the easy way out of difficult challenges. I wonder how many times I've missed a blessing that God had in store for me. To the contrary, I've found that doing the right thing, sometimes the harder thing, often takes supernatural strength that only the Lord can provide. It also requires initiative on our part. That's where obedience comes into play.

If I had known what this storm would entail, I would have done everything in my power to avoid it. It's been difficult. But, like choosing to run in the Christmas race, I would have missed the blessings.

James 1:2-4 tells us,

Consider it pure joy, my brothers and sisters, whenever you face trials of many kinds, because you know that the testing of your faith produces perseverance. Let perseverance finish its work so that you may be mature and complete, not lacking anything.

The foregoing verses are hard for me to fathom. Does it make sense to be joyful when you go through trials, when your faith is tested? It seems counterintuitive but it's in the Bible and I've seen this truth play out in my own life. While I wouldn't have chosen this storm, and it's been painful at times, I've seen God do some amazing things.

It's strange to say but, had I not gone through the trials of the past several years, I would have missed a number of blessings. Spending time in His Word and in prayer have been richer. I've met people who have encouraged me and spoken wisdom into my life. Many of these individuals are now close friends. My heart is softer towards the elderly. And while I am so far from where I need to be spiritually, this storm has humbled me, made me less self-reliant, and hopefully more God-reliant. Despite the difficulties and the pain, I am grateful.

While I don't understand the big picture, it doesn't matter. He is God, I am not. And He is doing something bigger. Nothing is wasted when God is in it. I am the living proof.

During those times when I've been ready to give up, to just throw in the towel, He has sent the right people into my life and also encouraged me with His Word. Galatians 6:9 is a verse I have committed to memory:

Let us not become weary in doing good, for at the proper time we will reap a harvest if we do not give up.

And Colossians 3:23-24 reminds me,

Whatever you do, work at it with all your heart, as working for the Lord, not for human masters, since you know that you will receive an inheritance from the Lord as a reward. It is the Lord Christ you are serving.

When things get tough, when others criticize, or when I second-guess myself (which I do continually), I'm reminded that I am serving Him. His strength is perfect in my weakness. He is more than enough.

Looking back, signing up for the Christmas race and deciding to run it was not a mistake. God had something more to teach me. And though it had its difficulties, finishing the race, not giving up, was rewarding. I'm better for having run it.

Robert Jones

Lord, I believe that caring for my parents, despite this storm, is a divine calling. Thank You for the people You have sent into my life to encourage me. Thank You for that "extra gear" You have given me on the challenging hills. My desire and prayer, above all, is that You would give me the wisdom and strength to finish well, all for Your honor and glory. Amen.

Chapter 1: The New Normal

In the Lord I take refuge.

Psalm 11:1

I n the state of Illinois there is a city called, "Normal." I've never been there but it sounds like the kind of place I'd like to live. I don't know about you, but I love "normal," meaning what is comfortable, routine, stable, predictable.

There's a sense of contentment with the normal life, whatever that is for each of us. Being a "Type A" personality, I've carefully planned my life to be "normal." However, somewhere along the way I have lost the sense of what "normal" is supposed to look like.

I'm still adjusting to "what is" versus "what was." It's surreal for sure but perhaps not a bad thing. Reflecting on what was, I realize now that I was too comfortable being comfortable.

I have a hunch that most people don't live "normal" lives, despite how they appear. I know that my assertion is a generalization but, the more I get to know people, the more I realize that everyone is going through something. When someone asks, "How are you doing?" we often reply, "I'm fine." But often, our response to that question hides something deeper. We don't want to reveal the fact that sometimes we are not "fine," especially as professing followers of Jesus Christ. I'm often guilty of this. I don't like attention, nor am I comfortable being vulnerable, and admitting that I don't have it all together. I wonder what it would look like if we were honest, if I were honest.

Trials are no respecter of people and they affect each of us at some point. The Bible is very clear on this truth. Sure, like everyone I've had my share of "storms" but, looking back, I really can't complain; life overall has been pretty smooth up until a few years ago. I came to know Jesus Christ in my early thirties, and He changed my perspective from one of a skeptic and pessimist to a "glass half full" person. But this storm has given my faith a reality check. I should have paid more attention to what the Bible says about tough times. I was unprepared for the things to come...

The reality is, there are things in life which we cannot control, perhaps most things. The second part of Matthew 5:45 tells us that we will experience trials in this life. "He causes His sun to rise on the evil and the good, and sends rain on the righteous and the unrighteous."

It was easy for me to view the past with rose-colored glasses. Life seemed somewhat "normal" until the year 2020. Then came an unprecedented, devastating pandemic which affected all of us in some way. Sickness, death, isolation, division… So many people experienced tragic loss, and we, as a society, are still reaping the consequences of that horrible disease. I don't believe that life will ever be the same and we've been living in a "new normal" as a society since then, in my opinion. Concurrently, 2020 also began a year of personal loss for me: the year that I watched my father start to go downhill, cognitively and physically. And his decline would come to a head at the end of 2022 and then climax in 2023.

I initially chose "The Long Goodbye" as the title for this book because it described my experience perfectly. At that time, I realized that I had lost the Dad I knew. A stroke in 2011 and a more serious one in 2016 had done their worst to my father. Obvious signs of decline became evident, and it was heartbreaking to watch.

My original goal was to write about my experiences with Dad, so the title seemed perfect. But circumstances changed and caused me to come up with something different. First of all, a number of other authors have used "The Long Goodbye" as a title and I didn't want this to be just another book about cognitive decline and caring for an elderly parent. What would be the point? I can't provide any expertise on the subject because I have none. One thing that is clear to me though is sadly this: the disease affects many people and there is no cure. If you're reading this you probably know someone, perhaps close to you, who suffered or is suffering from some form of Alzheimer's disease or dementia. My purpose was to tell Dad's story and how God saw us through the storm. My prayer was to encourage others who might be going through a similar situation. I wanted to share my experience and let people know that I found hope in the midst of the storm. Without the message of hope, there would be no need for this book.

Then something happened that changed everything. While I was focused on Dad's condition and well-being, my mother's physical and cognitive health took a completely unexpected, serious downward turn. Now I had two parents, who lived five hours from me, with major health issues. Consequently, the title kind of wrote itself: If it were just Dad...

Things went progressively downhill for Dad in 2022, culminating in major crises at the end of the year. I hoped and prayed that 2023 would be different, and it was in some ways, but the "wins" were replaced with new challenges. I never questioned my faith but sometimes wondered where God was in all of this, and what His purpose was, especially when the struggles seemed insurmountable. In the heart of the storm, I often prayed these words from the Psalms: "How long, Lord?" A former pastor of mine often quoted the last part of 2

Chronicles 20:12, which I also prayed continually: "We (I) do not know what to do, but our (my) eyes are on you."

At times I would see light at the end of the proverbial tunnel but typically it would be one step forward and five back. Many times, I faced situations of "hurry up and then wait." For many months that was the rhythm of life for me.

At the close of 2024, heading into the year 2025, the storm has calmed somewhat but it's not over. There are "good days and bad days" and often things are unpredictable. Looking ahead, I don't know what the future holds. But looking back from the other side, I clearly see the hand of God, strengthening and guiding me. There have been too many instances of miracles and blessings which cannot be explained apart from divine intervention.

Incredibly, in early 2023, it took just a few months to sell Mom and Dad's twenty-plus acre farm in Virginia. Concurrently, we were able to get Dad into a memory care facility in Pennsylvania and purchase a home for Mom close to us. Experts told us that these things would take much longer. God's timing was miraculous and perfect. The "train" was moving so quickly that I didn't appreciate all He was doing at the time. But I can see it now and want to give Him all of the glory for what He has done.

I am so thankful that we were able to move Dad into Mom's new home for the remaining months of his life. God not only provided the wisdom, strength, and resources for everything, but He also raised up so many wonderful, compassionate people along the way to help us. But that's what He has done all of my life, even in my younger years when I was running away from Him. For that, I am eternally grateful.

God has been working all along in this storm, in His perfect will and timing, and He continues to do so. The difficult thing for me has been that most things didn't happen according to my timing. It was hard to see a way out when the tempest was raging, and I couldn't see beyond the darkness. But He never let go of me (or my parents). Psalm 27:14 (and many other Bible verses) reminds me that I need to wait on Him and His perfect timing: "Wait for the Lord; be strong and take heart and wait for the Lord."

I don't believe that any of us like to go through trials or suffering. Some hard times can be caused by our own bad decisions and choices (I'm living proof of that) but some can only be explained as part of living in this fallen world. And there is an enemy who would like nothing better than to take us down (see 1 Peter 5:8). Through it all I need to continually turn to God's Word, the inerrant, wonderful Holy Bible, to be continually reminded of these things. Romans 12:12 declares, "Be joyful in hope, patient in affliction, faithful in prayer."

I am so grateful that I no longer have to make the grueling five-hour trips to southern Virginia, often at a moment's notice, to deal with crises which seemed to surface on a daily basis. Thankfully Mom now lives just three miles from me. She has much better medical care than she had in rural Virginia and there are more opportunities to socialize. But challenges remain. She has memory and physical issues and there is no silver bullet for a permanent cure. Medicine, injections, chiropractic, and physical therapy help to alleviate the pain and keep her conditions at bay. But the situation is very fluid. Still, I thank God for the good moments we have.

Dad was still with us when I wrote a significant portion of this book in mid-2023, so I refer to him often in the present tense. Sadly, after his long, courageous battle with vascular dementia, he finally succumbed to the disease on September 26, 2023. Although the Lord gave us several months of "extra time" and I have no regrets, I still miss him terribly. Even though he's been gone for almost a year-and-a-half, it's all still very "new" and I haven't fully come to terms with it. Yet I rejoice in the fact that he "finished well" and my hero is now in the presence of His Savior, the Lord Jesus Christ.

Obviously more storms will come in this life, Jesus told us as much in John 16:33. But the second part of that verse tells me to take heart because Jesus Christ has overcome the world. It's the joy and inner peace He gives which have allowed me to survive this storm and hopefully be drawn closer to my Savior.

The experiences over the past several years would have been the end of me, if not for God. I would not have written this book if it weren't for the indescribable peace and joy that only the Lord Jesus Christ can bring. I love Philippians 4:6-7 which is a constant reminder of His presence:

Do not be anxious about anything, but in every situation, by prayer and petition, with thanksgiving, present your requests to God. And the peace of God, which transcends all understanding, will guard your hearts and your minds in Christ Jesus.

Over the past several years I have held onto that peace like a life preserver. I pray that you will experience His peace and presence in whatever you may be going through.

I'm still trying to figure out what "normal" looks like. But if it means drawing me closer to the God who loves me, saved me from a life of sin and spiritual death and is intimately involved in my life, I'm all in.

Chapter 2: Dad and Mom

"Honor your father and mother"—which is the first commandment with a promise— "so that it may go well with you and that you may enjoy long life on the earth."

Ephesians 6:2-3

Each day is a gift from God. No matter our age, social status, education level, income, it makes no difference; no one is guaranteed another second, let alone another day of life. Most friends my age no longer have living parents. I am grateful and consider myself blessed to have parents who lived into their eighties.

I love my mom and dad dearly. I have the utmost respect for them. If that were not true, I would not have taken on the role of primary caregiver when they could no longer care for themselves. But I need to be honest and don't want to give anyone the wrong impression: I did not have a storybook childhood, and I do carry some emotional scars. I also lived a very sinful lifestyle, especially in my teenage years. The older I get and the more I get to know people, I've learned that there are many who have similar or worse experiences growing up. That said, I owe everything to my parents and would not be the man I am if not for their love, wisdom, and example.

My parents received a great deal of press in my first two books (*Average Man* and *Family Love Letters*) so some of this information is duplicative. However, it's germane to the story so I'm including it here.

Dad was born in south Jersey and Mom in Philadelphia. They met while Dad was home on leave from the Air Force and the rest, they say, is history. They wed in a small south Jersey church, in the same town where Mom grew up. They were married for more than sixty-three years before Dad left this earth. As it turned out, my wife and I were also married in that same church in the mid-1980s.

Dad had an impressive career in the Air Force, but I didn't know much about his military service until the past several years. In fact, I didn't know much at all about his early life. When I was growing up, Dad kept to himself and was hard to get to know. He had a temper and I tested it a number of times. When he would take off his belt, I knew that I was in trouble. As a child I didn't always hear positive feedback from Dad, in fact, I often heard just the opposite. But Dad pushed me to be the best I could be and, especially as I got older, expressed his esteem for me. Interestingly, I know that he "talked me up" when I was growing up because I heard positive things from Dad's friends and colleagues.

At my request he wrote his personal story ("Reflections on my Journey of Life") in 2016, just before his second stroke. This simple, well-written, twelve-page document gave me a better understanding of Dad's heart and personality. It is one of my most prized possessions. Dad and I grew really close over the years, especially the past several. Since the strokes and dementia affected Dad's health, he opened up and disclosed things I never knew about him. As hard as the past few years have been I am so grateful for the way I got to know Dad. I praise God for that.

I share the same first name as Dad, but my middle name reflects my late maternal grandfather's (Pop) first name. Pop was a significant influence in my life, and I carry his name proudly. He went home to be with the Lord in January of 1997, on my younger brother's birthday. Whenever Pop would write letters to me, he always annotated the local temperature in the upper right-hand corner. Consequently, each morning I write the current temperature in my journal. By doing so, not a day goes by when I don't think of him.

When I was growing up, my parents, siblings, grandparents, aunts, uncles, and cousins all referred to me as "Robbie," or "Rob" for short. Personally, I never cared for those nicknames. When I started attending school, teachers and classmates referred to me as "Bob," and that is how most people know me today. That nickname was good enough for Dad, so it's good enough for me. Only my immediate family calls me "Rob" these days.

It's not an exaggeration to say that Dad grew up with very little. I could never begin to understand the level of poverty and hardship he endured in his early years. To look at him, you would never know about his humble beginnings. He worked hard as a teen and adult and made something of himself. I wasn't aware of how he was raised because he never talked nor complained about his upbringing or circumstances. However, I strongly believe that difficult experiences from his childhood and teen years affected who he was as a husband and father. Some of those character traits were positive, others not so much.

Dad was one of six children. A seventh child, a sister, died at birth. He served our country proudly and worked two jobs as long as I can remember. Mom is an only child, raised by two Godly parents. She was a stay-at-home Mom until I was a teenager and held various sales jobs over the years. Mom, and especially Dad, had extremely strong work ethics which rubbed off on my siblings and me.

I am the oldest of three children. I have a younger sister and brother. My parents raised us in a small, three-bedroom ranch house in South Jersey, a few miles from Philadelphia. When I was a junior in high school Dad moved us to a middle-class neighborhood about eight miles from our original home. All of my early memories from childhood and teen years, both good and bad, are of time spent in south Jersey. Although I've lived in south-central Pennsylvania for over thirty years, I'm still "from New Jersey."

I was not raised in a Christian home, nor a particularly moral home. I won't get into the details but will only say this: I had no clue what a healthy marriage nor follower of Jesus was supposed to look like. Significantly, I had no understanding of the love, grace, and mercy of God. Ultimately each one of us is responsible for our own actions and I've had to confess and repent of my many past sins. However, much of what we learn from our parents is more "caught than taught" and we can easily model bad behavior if our moral compass is distorted.

Mom was easy-going but, as I said, Dad was strict and meted out the most discipline on me as the oldest. I didn't help matters by my rebellious behavior and gutter language, especially in my teens. While I often deserved what I got, Dad sometimes took out his punishment on me in anger. I feared Dad, but looked up to him with respect. That is true to this day. While some of my childhood memories are negative, I choose to remember the positive things about Dad and our relationship, especially in my adult years when Dad's heart softened. Dad was no worse a sinner than I was/am and Jesus redeemed him just as He did me. That is what is so amazing about God's grace!

It's interesting how we view life when we're younger. Dad was very tough physically and I not only feared him but also looked up to him as a strong protector. Ironically, he was short in stature, something I didn't think about until I was an adult. In high school when he ran track he was known as "the little engine that could..." Yet he was the strongest man I know, bigger than life to me, growing up.

If it weren't for Dad, I would have played the clarinet or perhaps not pursued music at all. He insisted that I take up the saxophone in fourth grade, which ultimately opened up many professional and ministry opportunities in music. If it weren't for Mom and her encouragement, I may not be a follower of Jesus Christ. If it weren't for Dad, I may not have gone to Texas where I met my wife and began a thirty-six-year career which provided for my family. If it weren't for Mom, I may not have a compassionate side. One other thing about Dad: while he could be short-tempered at times, he took good care of Mom whenever she was sick or had to be hospitalized. It's something that stands out to me now. I owe a lot to my parents and cling to the good memories, especially over these past several years.

Dad was a very smart man, much more intelligent than I am. He was a tireless worker, financial expert, handyman and even a published poet.[1] No job was ever beneath him to provide for himself and his family. Yet he never boasted about his accomplishments. It was heartbreaking when the strokes and memory issues diminished his abilities. He supported me

---

[1] Months before Dad passed, I asked if I could someday publish some of his poetry. He agreed. Consequently, I have included one of his poems at the end of this book.

in my music, education, and family. He also taught me how to be generous, something which I do my best to model in my relationship with Jesus Christ. Starting in my college years we grew closer, although Dad mostly kept to himself and was never a man of many words. I would not have taken the path I did in life if not for Dad's support. Despite anything that happened in the past, he was my biggest fan and always my hero.

Significantly, Dad did not display a great deal of emotion when I was younger. I was taught that men do not cry, which was a struggle for me during times when I felt pain. The first time I saw Dad display real emotion, besides anger, was when I started my career in Texas back in 1983. Dad had driven me from New Jersey to Texas and Mom flew in a few days later to join us. After my first day at work, we said our goodbyes, and Mom broke into tears and Dad did the same.

I had never seen him cry and frankly didn't know how to handle it. It was the beginning of the softening of his heart, which really became evident after our first child was born. It was also a catalyst for the softening of my heart which ultimately led me to Christ.

Of course, as Dad's health deteriorated over the past several years, he became very vulnerable and emotional— which were not necessarily bad things but definitely a change from the past.

Without question, one of the nicest things Dad ever did for me happened in 1983. I was living and working in

Texas, just out of college. I met my future wife, Diane, in our employer's intern program, and we started dating after knowing each other only several days. After a few months I asked her to marry me. Dad was the only family member I informed about our engagement, which says something about how our relationship and trust had grown.

Dad bought airline tickets and flew Diane and me to their home in south Jersey for Thanksgiving as a surprise for my mother. Dad had never met Diane, so I was moved by his faith in my choice of a fiancée, sight unseen! This speaks volumes about his trust in me and shows how much closer we had grown. Mom was totally surprised when I showed up for Thanksgiving with Diane. It's a testament to Dad's big heart and generous spirit, and a memory I'll cherish forever.

I also recall a time when Dad called me a few years into my marriage. He wanted to invest money for me to buy and manage a music store. I was humbled by his offer but graciously declined. I do not have the chops to run a business nor the desire to own a music store. I told Dad to save his money and use it for his life and needs. This gesture is yet another example of Dad's generous heart.

We weren't rich by American standards, but Dad provided everything my sister, brother, and me needed. He grew up in poverty, but I didn't realize that until I was older. Because of Dad's hard work and giving heart, I have never known what it is like to be in want. Dad wasn't around a lot during the week because he worked two jobs, but he taught me respect and personal responsibility.

After I was married in the early 1980s, Diane and I lived in central Jersey while Mom and Dad continued to live in south Jersey. We were only an hour away from my parents, so visits were frequent. In 1989 we relocated to south central Pennsylvania for a career opportunity and we remain there to this day. At that time, Diane and I lived less than three hours from my parents, which still allowed us to visit them often.

In the early 1990s, Mom and Dad made the decision to move from their south Jersey home to a twenty-plus acre property in southern Virginia. Dad retired early due to stress experienced in his career. His retirement dream was to buy a big piece of land and raise some farm animals in the country. To that end he and Mom had purchased several properties in Virginia before deciding to settle on one in a very rural area. They would spend more than thirty years there before the "storm" hit.

As a boy, Dad spent time on his aunt's farm when my paternal grandparents lost their home. Dad and his sister actually lived in what amounted to a chicken coop, with no running water nor amenities. Despite the humble circumstances he had to endure, Dad appreciated the simplicity of farm life. He always dreamed of having land and farm animals himself. Mom especially grew tired of the Jersey traffic, cost of living and taxes, and so she embraced the idea of living in the country. Looking back, I believe that I would not be writing this story had they not made the decision to move so far away from family. Their decision to remain there as their health waned would exacerbate the storm we would experience.

My wife and I didn't fight my parents' decision to relocate so far away because of concerns about Dad's health at the time. He had a highly stressful career as well as a second job he worked at night. The day-to-day grind took a noticeable toll on him as time went on. These are my parents, who provided for and raised me. If this move was their retirement dream, who was I to stand in the way?

While I respected their decision to move and live the life they wanted, I secretly disagreed with it for several reasons. First, they would be approximately five hours from me and even farther from my brother and sister. Second, care of the farm, which consisted of horses, donkeys, goats, chickens, guinea hens, a turkey and a llama, would tie them down. This precluded vacations and limited visits with their children and grandchildren. It would also become unsustainable as they aged.

We felt that Mom and Dad could have bought property anywhere close to their children. But cost of living, taxes, and climate played a role in their decision to move to southern Virginia. Based on the rural location and lack of services, their place reminded me of the old "Green Acres" television show. I often joked that my parents didn't live at the end of the earth, but one could see it from there! But again:

these are my parents and I couldn't stand in their way. I could only voice my opinion while respecting their decision.

Mom had this idea that the family would visit often, ride her horses, and enjoy an idyllic life with them on the farm. But that idea never came to fruition. My siblings and I had families of our own. Our children were involved in music, sports, and school-related activities which kept us close to home. That coupled with our careers made it difficult to make the five-plus hour trip. The distance made me appreciate the close proximity of my grandparents and relatives growing up. It seems that this scenario is more of the exception than the rule these days.

For my wife and me, most of our visits over the years were tied to holidays and vacations. As much as we kept in touch through letters and phone calls, I feel that Mom and Dad missed a lot of our kids' (their grandkids') lives. Don't get me wrong; they were wonderful grandparents for my children. They loved life on the farm, and we enjoyed many visits over the years. But they sacrificed precious time with family. Sadly, there are some things you can't get back but thankfully, God meets us where we are and can create beauty out of anything.

Over the years, especially the last ten, I continually discussed the future with my parents and the necessity to have a "Plan B" in place. In the back of my mind, I had a growing concern that their living conditions would eventually become unsustainable as they aged. As time went by, they dropped hints that I would be responsible for their affairs if/when "something would happen." As their sixtieth and especially seventieth birthdays were celebrated, I encouraged (and progressively pleaded with) them to downsize and consider relocating to a smaller property, closer to the kids, while their health was still good. The care of large farm animals was especially concerning to me. Mom's response was always, "I know. Someday we'll do that. We're fine, we can handle things on our own." Those words would come back to haunt them (and me) as "someday" would arrive with a vengeance, especially starting in early 2022.

Dad had so much energy in his mid-fifties. He created multiple pastures, constructed every board of fencing and animal lean-tos, fed and cared for the farm animals, and even taught full-time at a high school in Virginia. Not only was he a drivers Ed teacher but he also handled the finances for the school. I don't know how he found time nor the energy to do it all! It was impressive.

Mom worked from home selling office supplies, something she enjoyed and at which she was greatly skilled. Life seemed to be "normal" in Virginia until I got the call from Mom in 2011: "You'd better get down here; Dad had a stroke and was taken to a hospital in Lynchburg." As a mid-level manager in a large organization, I was about to host a critical two-day meeting with clients from around the world. I dropped everything to hurry home, pack a bag, and then headed to Virginia where I spent the next week. Each day I drove Mom to the hospital, over an hour from her home, to visit Dad. I quickly learned how to feed and care for the farm animals while Dad was hospitalized and then at home to recover. Dad's ability to care for the farm became limited and would soon be gone altogether. Before I returned home to Pennsylvania, Mom took over the primary responsibilities for the animals' care.

Being away from my family was distressing. As a manager, missing work and catching up with a backlog was also stressful. Dad lost some physical capacity from the stroke but thankfully gained a significant amount of it back over the next several years. This was the time when he became much more emotional than ever. His emotions would become more fragile as the years went by.

We enjoyed several years of relative peace until April of 2016, just before Easter, when Dad had a second stroke. This one was much worse than the first as Dad lost significant physical and cognitive abilities. Dad had a stubborn side; he refused to seek medical care when he began to show signs of a stroke. After a few days he knew something was wrong and insisted on calling an ambulance. I sometimes wonder if things would have turned out differently had he gone to the hospital right away.

After a brief hospital stay, he spent a week in a rehab center which was not the best experience. He was an extreme fall risk and limited in what he could do. He hated being there and became uncooperative with the facility. Eventually I had to have him released early. Still, he is a fighter and defied the doctors as he eventually resumed driving, though I worried constantly about his abilities to be on the road. The damage from the stroke not only affected Dad's physical and cognitive abilities, but also his speech and ability to express himself.

I spent the better part of a month with Mom and Dad in 2016, missing critical responsibilities with my family and career. I continued to plead with my parents to consider downsizing and relocating north, closer to family, for better medical care and support. Dad was no longer able to care for the farm and Mom did the best she could. But it was dangerous for her to be out in the pastures alone, carrying bales of hay, feeding the large animals, and lifting heavy water troughs. In addition, summers are extremely hot there, which made it dangerous to be exposed to the sun and heat for too long.

Specialized medical facilities and doctors all required a drive of an hour or more, making it difficult to receive needed care. There was no family living anywhere nearby, no support system, and few friends. Mom and Dad attended church early on but gave that up after a few years. A simple trip to the grocery store took more than twenty minutes each way. And their house was broken into at least once. For many, a severe stroke would have been a wake-up call for changes, but Mom believed that "they were fine" and refused to make changes. So, things continued as they were in Virginia, at least for them. But my responsibilities and increased concern for my parents were just beginning. I now needed to check on them often to ensure that they were safe.

Dad was more aware than Mom of their situation. At one point after the big stroke in 2016, Dad called and asked me to find property for them in Winchester, Virginia. Dad wanted to remain in Virginia but closer to the kids. Winchester is a larger town with services and medical care, but also has plenty of open land for the rural feel they were accustomed to. Moreover, the distance is much shorter from my home and would allow for better support from me and more frequent visits from family. Dad astutely recognized that life could not go on like this. Mom, not so much…

I was grateful for Dad's initiative and thought that this would be ideal for everyone. We secured a real estate agent and had land selected where my parents could still enjoy farm life but on a smaller scale. Additionally, I could be at their place within an hour in case of an emergency. But Mom got cold feet. She said, "Dad cannot move, it would kill him." I look back now and think, "If only they had moved when they had the chance…" But again, it's not helpful to live life looking back at "if-onlys" or "what ifs." As it turned out, we would end up moving Dad eventually—in 2023, under less-than-ideal circumstances.

Over the next several years I continually pleaded with my parents to consider downsizing and moving to a more practical home. Mom continued to refuse, stating: "We're fine, we'll know when it's time." Deep down I believed that this was not going to end well. I was reminded of a quote attributed to Martin Luther: "Not now becomes never."

At one point, Mom considered moving to Florida. She was communicating with friends and real estate agents who enticed her to relocate to the "Sunshine State." I would have supported them moving to a retirement community in Florida where they would have a support system. Anything to get away from the responsibilities on the farm. But Mom was never serious, and this became a pipe dream. As I stated, I could not force my parents to relocate but the time would come when there was no choice, and mom would beg to move...

After the 2016 stroke I was at a crossroad. Due to Dad's condition and the help my parents required I was not certain of the future. There were so many unknowns. I had missed so much work that it affected my employees and the organization. And once again, I was away from my family for extended periods. By God's provision, I was eligible to retire from my career, but it was not the best time for us financially. Also, from a personal standpoint, I still considered myself young and was not ready to leave my career at that time. But what could I do? My parents needed help. If not me, then who? I prayed and sought counsel from a Christian brother who spoke wisdom into my life. After a great deal of prayer and soul-searching, I retired from my first career in July of 2016 to be more available to my parents.

In spite of second-guessing, doubts, and some fear, retiring at that time was the right thing to do. I believe with all of my heart that God worked everything out in His perfect timing, and I praise Him for that. I was eventually hired as a part-time consultant which provided for us financially and facilitated frequent visits to my parents'. The job was flexible, and my employer was very understanding which allowed me to visit my parents to help with medical appointments and little jobs around the farm. After the contract on that job was terminated, I was off for several months and then offered another flexible contractor job which I worked for the better part of three years. My sister and brother, both younger than I, have careers and families of their own, making visits difficult for them. I respected that and believed that God had arranged things in my life to be available for my parents at such a time as this. Things were manageable for me and my parents, for the time being.

At the beginning of 2020 I started to notice significant changes in Dad's health. He was having difficulty putting thoughts and sentences together. He also became very emotional, confused, forgetful, and irrational at times. He was still managing his finances and able to drive short distances, but the cognitive decline became more obvious.

I made the decision to retire from my contractor job in January of 2020 as I saw things developing in Virginia. My goal was to visit my parents once per month to help them out. Personally, I also desired to pursue writing, teach Sunday School, and start a music ministry in assisted living/nursing homes. This seemed like a great plan for my "Chapter 2!" And then the pandemic hit, killing my plans and curtailing visits due to government restrictions on travel. Still, I managed to make several trips to Virginia for Mom and Dad's medical appointments and to help around the farm. And with the Lord's guidance, and a great editor, I was able to write two books and ghost-write another for a friend. But the storm which had been simmering for several years would now gradually intensify.

There are times when I wonder how I ended up in this storm. I never raised my hand and said, "Hey Mom and Dad, pick me to be your "point man!" This is not how I planned out my life. As a follower of Jesus Christ, I had a heart to serve people and looked forward to ministry opportunities near my home. I had also hoped to travel and do things Diane and I couldn't do when we had full-time careers. But God had other plans. It has been said that we should write our plans in pencil and give God the eraser. That saying has certainly played out over the past several years. I carry around a big eraser. Proverbs 16:9 supports this truth: "The heart of man plans his way, but the Lord establishes his steps."

As the oldest and the one my parents called on when help was needed, I became the focal point for supporting them. This responsibility was augmented as their health declined and needs increased. I've heard it said that "God doesn't call the qualified, He qualifies the called." This was true in my case. I was certainly not qualified and felt totally inadequate for the responsibilities I had to take on. But this was what my parents wanted. I totally relied on the Lord to help me navigate this storm. I did my best but still doubted myself continually.

Being a caregiver, care manager, and agent for my parents has been one of the hardest things I've ever had to do. Initially, I embraced the idea and believed (and still do) that God called me to do it. Being totally honest, I desired no credit or attention. My parents sacrificed so much for me and, Biblically, I could do no less for them. I was compelled and privileged to look out for their interests, keep them as safe as possible, and ensure that their health was maintained. But just being transparent: there have been and still are times where I've been ready to walk away. And if I didn't have Jesus, I'm certain that I would have taken an easier path in lieu of the role I took on.

There is a myriad of books on elder care and dementia, but I've learned that every situation is different, and one size does not fit all. I've talked to enough doctors, nurses, memory care staff, and attorneys to know that every case is unique. I've also heard a saying which goes something like, "If you've seen one case of dementia, you've seen one case..." If I had to describe it in one word it would be, "unpredictable." No one has a corner on this market, in my opinion. And I've learned that it is a road you cannot travel alone.

Importantly, I try to seek the Lord in every situation and prayerfully make decisions. He has provided wisdom and direction when I've needed it most. I also seek the counsel of trusted medical and legal experts. I'm so grateful for the people the Lord has brought across my path, not only the professionals, but friends who have had the right words when I needed them.

In 2022, Dad's condition took a noticeable turn for the worst. If that wasn't enough, in early 2023 things would go unexpectedly wrong with Mom. It was tantamount to getting punched in the face and then in the gut.

Dementia is a terminal disease and took a horrible toll on Dad. Gone was the tireless man who could manage finances and fix anything. Gone was the man who could walk and use the bathroom, without assistance. Gone is the man who could tell me, "Things will be okay, Rob, don't worry about it." Yet God still brought beauty in the midst of ashes.

I cried a lot over the past few years, and little things still make me weep, because it's been a long goodbye to the man I once knew. Yet there was something mellow and sweet about him as he lived his final months "in the moment." I consider it a precious gift that we received extra days with him where we enjoyed some lucid, meaningful times. But towards the end those moments became few and far between. While it doesn't seem real at times, there is a level of acceptance to what "is" and not what "was." Every person on this earth is a creation of God and deserves dignity and respect. My goal was to honor Dad in that way until he was called home to be with Jesus.

If it were just Dad, things would be difficult enough. But then there was Mom who has a harder time with what "is." She went through an unbelievable time of back and leg pain, and most of that condition is not curable. Those physical issues still affect her daily living, and I don't pretend to understand the level of her pain. If that weren't enough, she also suffers from memory issues which manifest themselves in irrational and sometimes negative speech and behavior. I try to be empathetic due to the trauma she's been through, but sometimes it is challenging. Still, as difficult as things have been, I believe that God worked many miracles to bring us to this point. I have to continually remind myself that this is not the Mom I knew and things are not as either of us planned. But I am doing what she asked me to do and what is best for her health and well-being. Sadly, she has difficulty remembering all that transpired which led us to this point. I need the Lord to daily remind me to not take things personally. It's often easier said than done.

Throughout the storm I've asserted that, when Dad leaves this earth and is welcomed into heaven, I believe I will be sad but not for long. Why? Because I've grown close to him over the past two years of this long goodbye. We spent countless hours together, talking more openly than we ever have. And the time I've spent with him, in spite of the decline and changes to who he was, has been a priceless gift I wouldn't trade for anything. Most importantly, Dad made a confession of faith, trusting Jesus Christ for his salvation. I am so thankful to know that Dad is with His Lord and Savior and is no longer suffering from dementia.

The statement that "I won't be sad for long" turned out to be somewhat true, but his final days and ultimate passing still hurt and created a massive hole in my heart. Honestly, making funeral arrangements, dealing with finances and taxes, and ensuring that Mom is cared for left little time for grieving. Sometimes the loss of Dad will just hit me when I'm alone on a walk or lying in bed.

A few Christmases ago Dad gave me a hot lather shaving machine as a gift. Since his two strokes, Dad and I became much closer than we had been in earlier years. For birthdays and Christmas, he would seek out unique gifts like this for me. This gadget was not something I needed, nor would ever buy for myself. But it's one of my most cherished gifts from him. I think of him each day when I use this machine as part of my morning routine. I miss the phone calls, hearing his voice, telling me that "everything will be alright" when I encounter a tough situation.

On the wall in my office hangs a picture of Dad, when he was in his prime. In the photo he is wearing a flannel shirt, a winter vest, and work gloves. He was in a pasture, on his farm in Virginia, doing what he loved to do. We had copies of this photo reproduced for his memorial services. At the bottom of the picture is Hebrews 13:14 which reads: "For here we do not have an enduring city, but we are looking for the city that is to come." Dad knows that city now. I look forward to joining him there one day. And it's only because of Jesus…

Chapter 3: Signs of a Tempest

His thunder announces the coming storm; even the cattle make known its approach.

Job 36:33

It's Sunday May 26, 2024, in the middle of the night. There is a storm brewing. Thunder cracks in the distance, lightning illuminates the sky, wind is rocking the trees in the backyard. I'm uncomfortable when it gets like this. I don't like storms.

Several years ago, our house was struck by lightning—directly, in the middle of the night. It came as a surprise and sounded like a bomb exploding. Thankfully, there were no injuries nor fire. But the strike caused thousands of dollars in damage and repairs took months. The worst part of the incident was the fear and uncertainty when the strike occurred.

In 1993 after the big blizzard our basement flooded when the snow melted. This created a minor disaster. I don't like storms. I prefer peace.

God used the late Reverend Dr. Charles Stanley, among others, to draw me to Jesus Christ when I was hopelessly lost. I once heard Dr. Stanley say something like: "You're either in a storm, going into a storm, or coming out of a storm." I've come to learn that storms are a part of the journey we call "life" in this broken world. Jesus said in John 16:33 which I quote several times in this book. "I have told you these things, so that in Me you may have peace. In this world you will have trouble. But take heart! I have overcome the world." I have found great comfort in that verse which has proven to be true, over and over again in my life. I have found and am finding peace in this storm, moment-by-moment, day-by-day, in Jesus Christ.

As a Sunday School teacher and worship leader, one of the things I continually profess publicly is that God has always been faithful. Always. He has never failed me. Ever. Granted, things happen and I may never understand the reasons why in this lifetime. But through every "storm" God has taught me something. I know that there is a purpose in what I have gone through, and I'd like to think that I've grown in my walk with Jesus Christ.

It hasn't been easy, and I am 100% human which means very imperfect. Therefore, sometimes it takes me awhile to find peace in the storm. But I'm thankful that He has held me closely in the midst of it. And I am so grateful that He did not show me what I would face beforehand. I don't know if I could have stood had I known how intense and painful it would be.

A pastor friend recently reminded me how our walk with Jesus Christ is a lot like God's call to Abraham. In Genesis 12 of the Bible God calls Abraham to "Leave the land he had always known." If I apply that to my own life, the land I've always known is tantamount to my comfort zone, which is what is "normal" and predictable. Our Lord went on to say, "Go from your homeland to a new land that I will show you." Wow, so Abraham was told to leave his comfort zone for the unknown. And Abraham stepped out in faith and ultimately God accomplished His purposes through this man. Now I'm not Abraham and was not called to such a lofty task, but I see similarities between his story and my story. I believe that God called and prepared me for this journey to support my parents in their time of need. But, like Abraham, I had no idea where I was going or what I would face. And that journey continues, powered by His strength. May Your will be done, Lord.

2020

After I retired from my second career at the beginning of 2020, Mom would call periodically and ask me to make the five-hour trip to do little jobs around her Virginia property. I would spend hours mowing grass and cutting brush in pastures, repairing fences, painting, and cleaning gutters. I would also drive mom and dad to appointments and stores as needed.

Mom was not driving due to diabetic neuropathy in her feet. Dad was limited in what he could do and not able to drive long distances, so Mom always set up her appointments around my schedule. I was now officially "retired" so I made myself available to make the long trips to southern Virginia. I am not handy at all, but necessity is the mother of invention. I found myself repairing and maintaining things I never thought possible. Truth be told, I felt good about serving my parents and accomplishing things for them. I hated being away from home but genuinely enjoyed the work.

During my visits I began to notice that Dad's cognitive abilities and memory were declining, gradually but significantly. I am not a medical expert, so I saw this as nothing more than normal aging. But it got to the point where it didn't take a professional to know that something bigger was going on. Dad began to behave in unpredictable ways. The unpredictability became one of the most difficult things to deal with. This was not the man I knew.

Since my parents lived so far away, isolated in a rural area, they were continually on my mind. I was concerned about their health and safety above all, but also how they were managing their household and farm. It was just the two of them, with no neighbors close by, so I asked Mom to text or call me first thing each morning. Once I heard from her, I knew that everything was "okay." To be honest, until I heard from her each morning I could not relax.

In January, almost on cue after I retired from my contractor job, Mom called and told me that Dad was "all over the place" with his behavior. I didn't know what that meant but, as the year progressed, things became clearer: Something serious was happening to him and his decline was becoming very evident. The unpredictable behavior became the norm.

One prominent characteristic was that he was often at a loss for words, making it difficult to express himself. There were moments when we talked on the phone, and he sounded perfectly normal but more often than not he would fish for words and get frustrated when he couldn't express himself. That's the way it was for most of the year; there were ups and downs with regards to emotions, cognition, and behavior. Dad would not be formally diagnosed until early 2023 but the symptoms became clear as 2020 progressed. I just didn't realize the gravity of the situation and his doctors led me to believe that this was part of normal aging. No one would come out and say, "This looks like dementia."

In 2023 I learned from one of his friends that Dad would drive to the supermarket in a local town and ask for directions to get home. He would also forget how to start and shut off his vehicle. And he would leave lights on and water running around the house. Logical tasks became difficult. It was so not like him.

In February of 2020 I made an impromptu visit to Virginia after Dad called me. He had taken Mom to the Emergency Room (ER) for kidney, back, and abdominal pain.

I didn't realize it then, but her back pain would become a serious issue and a big part of this story in 2023. At some point, allegedly, Mom was in a pasture with her horses and took a spill, injuring her back and tailbone. On a daily basis she also lifted large bales of hay and periodically would dump out very heavy water troughs. Clearly, she over-exerted herself caring for the animals. I believe that over time these efforts exacerbated her back issues. Dad always worried about Mom's safety when he could no longer care for the farm. I was so focused on Dad that I never anticipated that Mom would develop serious health issues as well. But for now, this was just a distraction as most of the attention was on him.

Dad had a colonoscopy scheduled for July 1st. Diane and I drove down to Virginia the day before in preparation for his trip to the hospital the following day. At one point Dad had annual colonoscopies due to a history of colon cancer and rapidly-developing polyps. His gastroenterologist told me that Dad was a "polyp factory" because they formed so quickly. The doctor said that he had never seen anything like it! Understandably, we were praying for good results.

I drove Dad and Mom to the hospital for the procedure while Diane stayed back at their house. Due to Covid restrictions, only Mom was allowed to go into the hospital with Dad after being temperature-checked. Fortunately, it was a nice day, and I sat outside with a good book—actually, "the Good Book!" Praise God, Dad did very well with the colonoscopy and the results were good. It would turn out to be his last colonoscopy. Diane and I spent a few more days with my parents and had a wonderful visit.

On July 3ʳᵈ, after a nice breakfast with Mom and Dad, Diane and I headed back to Pennsylvania. Until now we had never had an issue with our vehicles, but this trip would be different. On this day our Jeep would become a casualty of the long, frequent trips to southern Virginia. We were making great time heading north on Interstate 81 towards Pennsylvania when something went wrong. I was approximately ninety miles from home, driving in the fast lane, when our Jeep Compass started making a strange noise. Then, several engine lights illuminated, and the vehicle began to slow down drastically. Miraculously, no one was beside me, so I was able to maneuver into the right lane as my speed went from seventy to ten miles per hour in a matter of seconds. I was grateful to make it safely onto the shoulder of the interstate. Although exits on this highway are usually miles apart, we just happened to be about 1000 feet from one. I practically had the accelerator to the floor, but we coasted to the exit ramp, onto a patch of dirt on the side of a road where the vehicle could go no further. I praised God that we were off of the busy highway. Even though it was extremely hot that day, we were safe and that's all that mattered.

Because it was Friday July 3ʳᵈ, many businesses were closed due to the Independence Day holiday. We called the auto club and had difficulty being connected to the right office. When we finally did get a local branch, we were told this: "Our vehicle could be towed back to Pennsylvania, but we could not be transported ourselves due to Covid restrictions." I pleaded with the auto club and said I'd even sign a waiver; we had to get home! They finally secured a driver who was willing to take us, but the wait was over two hours for the tow.

The heat notwithstanding, Diane and I had a good time sitting in the vehicle with the windows open as we waited for the tow truck. We had water and snacks and reminisced about the many blessings God has bestowed upon us, even though things in Virginia were becoming a challenge. At one point the driver called to get our specific location. After a while he pulled up in front of our Jeep and hooked it up.

The driver asked us to get into his truck while he dealt with getting our vehicle onto the flatbed. Diane and I had to walk through some high grass to get to the passenger side of the tow truck. When we sat down in the back seat, I noticed that each of us was covered with ticks! Lots of them! Why not! We both freaked out; Diane tried to remove them with a tissue, I was flicking them off and some landed on her! It was difficult to know if we had removed every tick, but we are still here so "no harm, no foul." We laugh about it now, but it was a little unnerving at the time!

When the driver had the vehicle secured on the flat bed, he insisted that one of us sit up front with him. I drew the short straw and made the ride back to Pennsylvania in the passenger seat. I do not do well in the front seat of vehicles, especially if I feel the driver is unsafe. He exceeded the speed limit for most of the journey and followed other cars a little too closely, in my opinion. Just being transparent, I was nervous.

When I was growing up, my late paternal grandfather ran a red light in downtown Philadelphia and we were hit on the passenger side, where I was sitting. I remember seeing the car coming at us and feeling helpless. Thankfully I only suffered from a bruised wrist, but the memories of that accident are still with me and I have a phobia about sitting in the front passenger seat of a vehicle.

I was so grateful that we made it home safely and that the tow was free based on our plan with the auto club. It appeared that we experienced a transmission issue, and we got our Jeep back from the shop after a few days. This event, coupled with the increasing long drives to my parents' place, led me to purchase a new, more reliable vehicle. I praise God for this because the trips to Virginia were about to become very frequent.

As the year progressed, Dad would periodically become impulsive and angry. He also suffered from depression, headaches, paranoia, and confusion. In addition to the memory and behavioral issues, Dad was also unsteady on his feet. I never saw him fall but at times he came close. As time went on, he did experience several falls when I was not there. I prayed continually for Mom and Dad, and for wisdom from the Lord. This was becoming much bigger than I could handle and I didn't know what to do. I asked God for strength to deal with whatever was to come.

Based on the phone calls and what I observed during my visits, I continued to plead with Mom and Dad to move. I've come to understand, and it makes perfect sense, that most people prefer to stay in their homes as long as possible. We as humans grow accustomed to what is familiar and comfortable. We also want to be independent and self-sufficient. I understood that and wanted what was best for Mom and Dad. So, my goal was always to respect their wish to remain in the home for as long as possible. But there are times when it is no longer practical or safe for elders to live in circumstances where harm can come to them. We were gradually but increasingly getting to that point. I could not envision a "happy ending" based on the direction this was headed. And little did I realize that cognitive and physical issues were simmering with Mom.

There are laws in place, and rightly so, to protect elders from abuse by their children and others. For that reason, no one can legally force parents from their homes, even with Power of Attorney (POA). One can pursue guardianship but, from my understanding, it is an expensive and cumbersome process where legal and medical professionals get involved. This was never on my radar for Mom and Dad; I respected their independence and wishes and prayed that they would make the right decisions to relocate when the time came.

Having said all of that, these three things have always driven my motivations with regard to my parents: their safety, health, and well-being, in that order. A fourth factor, their "happiness," was a bonus, but not always possible.

Periodically I would sit down with Mom and Dad and ask, "Given the circumstances, what do you want to do if things get out of hand and how can I help?" In 2020 they reiterated their collective response: "We want to stay in our house as long as we can." I would follow up with, "And what if/when you can no longer live alone and take care of yourselves?" Dad and Mom indicated that they would like to move close to me, not to show favoritism towards one child, but because I would be the one managing their personal and medical affairs. Their decision would place most of the responsibility on me, which was unnerving, but how could I say, "no?"

My parents gave me life and raised me. And I can't get past the fact that Jesus gave His life for me. In my spirit I believe that caring for them was and is the right thing to do. But it's not easy. And please understand that I am not judging anyone who makes the choice to not take on the role of caregiver. In fact, there are some who have told me that "I'm in over my head." In some ways I agree. But this is a personal decision between God and me, based on so many other factors. At least for now, I was available and convinced that this was the right thing to do.

In addition to POA responsibilities, my parents also assigned me to be the executor of their will. Dad even sent me a book on the subject so that I would know what I was getting into. Frankly, after reading that book, I concluded that the responsibilities would be overwhelming. Besides the amount of work, bureaucracies, and time, there is always the possibility of disgruntled family members. At this point in my life, I sought (and still hope for) simplicity and peace so these roles are not something I wanted. Dad especially was adamant about his decision to have me take care of Mom and their affairs, so I took his wishes very seriously. While I didn't feel like I was cut out for this, I was committed to doing my best, relying on the Lord for guidance, strength and wisdom. Practically, I prepared myself as much as possible by reading and seeking guidance from legal and medical experts. But I still felt very inadequate in this role.

I never envisioned that things would turn out the way they did. With circumstances the way they were, I believed that Mom and Dad would spend their golden years in southern Virginia. Consequently, I would be left dealing with the property and the animals after my parents were gone. I also never lost sight of the fact that my parents could outlive me as well.

Things could not have worked out more differently. Looking back, I believe that the Lord made things much easier than they could have been, at least from an administrative standpoint.

At this point my parents were relatively safe, in fair-to-good health, and in the place they wanted to be. But they were not necessarily "happy." Of course, happiness is dependent upon circumstances. What the Lord promises if we trust Him, are joy and peace. These are things which are not dependent upon our circumstances. That was my real hope for them: their personal peace and joy. Truthfully, I don't believe that they were experiencing either.

Dad, in his lucid years and even at this point, did not particularly like the idea of me making the long trips to help them. Let me be clear: He loved seeing me, but was concerned about my well-being. Dad did not want to impose on my life. I remember early in my marriage, when Dad still lived in south Jersey, he ended up in the hospital for what was thought to be a heart problem. Mom called to inform me of Dad's hospitalization but told me that he did not want me to know. I made the drive and showed up at the hospital anyway out of concern, but he was not pleased that I interrupted my life for him. He was not one for attention. He was selfless, until the day he left this earth.

To this day Mom will often lament about how "happy" she was living in southern Virginia. There is hardly a conversation where she will not bring up to anyone who will listen: "I miss my farm, I miss Virginia, I miss my animals, we should have never moved…" I can understand why she feels that way. She spent over thirty years in southern Virginia with Dad and we all enjoyed some happy times there. But Xanadu it was not. There were some difficult times over the years and not all of our memories are good ones. Sadly, Mom has forgotten the negative events which occurred there.

She forgets that she complained about the lack of services, lack of help, lack of family support, the medical care, taxes, and many other issues. The upkeep of the home and property also became overwhelming. And most significantly, Mom forgets that ultimately, she was totally incapacitated and alone. The situation became unsustainable and she understood that at the time. When things were at their lowest point in 2023, she begged to move. Sadly, she doesn't remember the details of what transpired in Virginia, leading to where we are now.

I can empathize with Mom because I tend to think fondly of life back in New Jersey when I was growing up. But while visits are nice whenever I go back, it's not the same as it used to be. Everything is different and I have no desire to live there again. That's the way life is, we live in seasons and things change. For me, I choose to hold onto the great memories and leave it at that. And "home" for me is not a geographic place, it is where my family is.

For now, while it was a sacrifice for me to make the five-hour drive and spend multiple days with my parents, it allowed them to be safe and at least where they wanted to be.

I had the time and availability and believe God called me to serve in this way. Jesus Christ gave everything for me. I knew that He would provide the strength and wisdom I needed to face whatever was to come. So, for now, we maintained the status quo. But things would ultimately devolve into a state of chaos.

Chapter 4: The Clouds Thicken

He makes clouds rise from the ends of the earth; He sends lightning with the rain and brings out the wind from His storehouses.

Psalm 135:7

In early 2021, during a visit to my parents' home in southern Virginia, I drove Dad to a local bank to set up an electronic funds transfer for him. He had been travelling to the bank, about twenty minutes away, several times a month, to deposit dividend checks from an investment account. With modern technology there was no reason to be making those trips, so I wanted to take that burden from him.

On the way to the bank, after several minutes of silence, Dad nervously said this to me: "Your mother and I are going to jail." The statement caught my attention, and I

Robert Jones

responded incredulously, "Dad, what are you talking about, what did you do?" He had trouble articulating it but, after a few probing questions, I surmised that Dad did not have everything together in order to prepare his tax returns. This was not like him at all. I then asked, "Dad, would you like me to take care of that for you?" When Dad gratefully answered "Yes," I knew that this was another sign of decline and it was hard for me to swallow.

Dad was a financial expert. He had always been on top of his personal affairs and helped a number of people get their budgets in order and out of debt. As a young boy, I learned the value of saving money from Dad. Out of respect, I never asked about his income, bills, or investments. Dad kept everything close to the vest and, moreover, it was really none of my business. But now he was willing to open up the books to me, out of desperation. I didn't see this coming, and my heart sank.

Back in 2016 when Dad had his second stroke and was in rehab, I took his records to the accountant who prepared my parents' tax returns. Although things were extremely complicated, thankfully Dad had everything in order. I am grateful that their accountant, who recently retired, was very familiar with my parents' financial records and past tax returns. Consequently, we were able to get the returns filed accurately and on time that year.

Now back to 2021: I knew that it would be a challenge for me to gather everything up from scratch and get the taxes done, especially since Dad's understanding was slipping. I found that his records were no longer in one place, and it was very difficult to get the paperwork together. More than that, it broke my heart that he was no longer able to handle this task that used to come so easily to him. I was stressed over all of this.

My parents had the foresight to visit a lawyer prior to Dad's decline. I knew nothing about POA and its importance, but learned quickly that it would be required to conduct business on my parents' behalf. Thank God that they made that decision. I now needed it in order to work with my parents' tax professional. As Mom and Dad's health declined, the durable POA became crucial to managing their finances, bills, and medical care. A little unsolicited advice to the reader: For future planning, it is wise to contact a trusted attorney who is familiar with Elder Law to discuss who would advocate for you in the event that you are no longer capable of handling both financial and medical matters. Things can happen quickly so there is no time like the present to be thinking about this.

One important thing I learned about POA is this: it does not give one carte blanche authority (for good reason) and it comes with a high bar of responsibility; one I take very seriously. I also learned the hard way that not every organization recognizes POA, especially certain government entities. I understand why there are rules in place, but some organizations have made it extremely difficult when it comes to helping elders who cannot make decisions themselves. I found this to be true even after Dad's death when it came to obtaining needed documents for tax preparation.

Be prepared to jump through some bureaucratic hoops but also be patient as you navigate the various systems. As an image-bearer of Jesus Christ I am continually reminded to be pleasant when dealing with people, even when a process becomes frustrating, and people aren't the friendliest. Sometimes the employees in these agencies are given a hard time by consumers so I try my best to encourage and lift them up, even when I hit administrative stumbling blocks. Colossians 4:5-6 reminds me: "Be wise in the way you act toward outsiders; make the most of every opportunity. Let your conversation be always full of grace, seasoned with salt, so that you may know how to answer everyone."

Having said all of that, POA has been absolutely essential for me to support and protect both of my parents, financially and medically. It is also well known, but worth repeating, that POA only applies to the living. When Dad passed, POA for him was no longer valid. When I represent Mom in financial, legal and medical matters, I must use her POA.

Because of the level of responsibility as well as personal integrity, I keep detailed records of everything I do. I share the information with Mom and did the same with Dad. Not only is this required, but it's also the right thing to do morally. Additionally, I don't even want to give the appearance of anything improper. At my parents' request, I don't share their financial or medical information with anyone else. That is what they asked me to do, and I am following their wishes. While I do my best to keep records of everything from medical to financial decisions, during the height of the storm, it became unwieldy to document every event and decision. Fortunately, most financial and medical records are available online which provides an accurate audit trail.

I continued to make frequent trips to southern Virginia in 2021 to help my parents with medical appointments and little jobs around their property. I can't tell you how many times I cut myself, pinched a finger, or hit my head walking into a donkey or horse lean-to building. I can laugh about it now, but I was the proverbial "fish out of water." I literally grew up across the river from the city of Philadelphia, so farm life was foreign to me and, frankly, not my cup of tea. But doing the work did give me satisfaction knowing that I was serving my parents. And I know that they appreciated it.

I was concerned that Dad was still driving as his abilities became limited. Fortunately, he wisely would only travel short distances. Mom told me that even the short rides became scary as Dad would drive very slowly and close to the shoulder of the road. His mental and physical capacities continued to decline gradually but noticeably. He had his share of good moments but often became frustrated and emotional when his memory failed, or he couldn't articulate his thoughts. He also had profound difficulty completing logical tasks. Sometimes he would say things like, "I don't know what to do next." These symptoms would become much more pronounced in 2022.

I realized that his lucid days were waning, so I was intentional about spending time with Dad. Looking back, this was a precious blessing from the Lord. I really enjoyed our time together and will cherish those memories forever. We talked a lot, much more than in the past. He shared things with me that he never would have in former years. It was obvious that God was doing a work in my father. This awful disease affected different parts of his faculties, but he could still remember things from the distant past. It was heartbreaking to watch his decline, but I feel like the Lord gave me a special gift to be able to spend so much time with him.

Calls from Mom were always an adventure. Usually when my phone rang and Mom was on the other end, something was going on in Virginia—and it wasn't good. One day during the summer she called to tell me that Dad cut his hand while trimming a shrub. This was a big deal because Dad was on blood thinners due to his two strokes. Evidently there was a great deal of bleeding, and he soaked a number of towels while driving himself to Urgent Care, thirty miles from his home. It took many bandages and eight stitches to close the wound. With Dad's memory issues he often took risks without thinking ahead about the possible consequences. I prayed that he learned his lesson and would no longer use the hedge trimmer.

I read a commentary by N.T. Wright on the Gospel of Mark. This sentence caught my eye, and I had not thought of this until now: "What do you do when the strong person in your life becomes weak?" This describes what was happening between Dad and me. Our roles were changing, and I was now helping care for the one who took care of me for so long…

My journal entries reflect what I was feeling and how I relied on the Lord for strength:

6/25/2021 – During the night, as I was anxious about my parents' health and inevitable future, You reminded me of Your peace. Thank You Lord.

11/5/2021 – Feeling a little numb this morning. Grateful for a nice visit with Mom and Dad, safe trip home. Once again, depressed about the situation down there and the what/when "ifs." I noticed a big difference in Dad's short-term memory and ability to come up with words. I got him on his computer, but he didn't know how to follow instructions; so not like him. The distance, the animals and their constant need for care, the property, "stuff," financial complexities… My biggest concern is that Mom and Dad are safe and cared for. Lord, I pray for strength and supernatural wisdom to not look at the circumstances but look to You. Please don't let it affect my health or Diane's. You have always been faithful. Thank You Father.

Little did I realize what lay ahead when I wrote the foregoing words in my journal. The what/when "ifs" would flood my life the following year. And it did affect my health to the point where at times I didn't think I would survive the stress. Throughout my life I feel like I have been pretty resilient, but I am not exaggerating: I experienced periods of dizziness, headaches, chest pain, fatigue, and feelings of hopelessness which I had difficulty controlling. I postponed medical appointments for myself due to close to twenty trips to Virginia in 2022, several of which were unplanned. Medical and legal professionals, as well as close friends, stressed the importance of self-care. I wish I had found a way to heed that crucial advice and take better care of myself. But during the heart of this storm things continually came up in Virginia which required immediate attention, so my priorities were shifted. Given the circumstances, right, wrong or indifferent, my parents came first.

Chapter 5: The Storm Begins

We are hard pressed on every side, but not crushed; perplexed, but not in despair; persecuted, but not abandoned; struck down, but not destroyed.

2 Corinthians 4:8-9

I'm so grateful that the Lord didn't reveal to me what would occur in 2022, especially towards the end of the year. I would have done everything I could have to prepare for and avoid what was about to happen. In retrospect, without God's grace, strength and wisdom, I literally would not have made it. Please understand the seriousness of this statement: I honestly would not have made it.

Looking back at my own life, I don't know how people who reject Jesus survive the trials and tribulations of this life. In my younger years, I turned to alcohol, drugs, relationships, education, career, anything I could to try and make sense of life, as well as numb the pain I hid inside. But at the end of the day those things did not satisfy. Only Jesus does.

The drive to my parents' place was long and often challenging due to traffic, the occasional wreck which would shut down roads, and inclement weather. A significant part of the trips included two-lane country roads. On a good day I could make it to southern Virginia between four and a half and five hours. The trips often left me exhausted and wondering how I would manage things. But there were blessings as well. I thank God for those He brought across my path during my travels.

My favorite stop along the way was a little coffee shop in the lovely town of Scottsville, Virginia. Baines Coffee and Books is about three hours from my home and became a regular stop, on the way to and from my parents' home. From the first time I walked into the establishment, Kristin, the staff, and local customers treated me like a friend. I love that I was referred to as their "long-distance regular!" The coffee, lattes, and pastries are still my favorite. But more significantly, this place was always an oasis for me in the midst of often difficult, stressful trips, when I didn't know what I would be facing with my parents. Kristin would always ask about Mom and Dad. She also graciously shared encouragement from her own life. Only God could orchestrate these friendships which I cherish to this day.

In the area where my parents lived, over the years I also became friends with staff at local businesses my parents patronized. Restaurants, the barber shop, the feed and hardware stores, and even area banks had employees who loved my parents. I could see why Mom and Dad were attracted to the area. These people were hospitable and became like family to me, especially when Dad's health deteriorated. Their encouragement, support, and kind words also helped me get through difficult times during this storm. Friends from the area still keep in touch with me to this day. I am also grateful for the encouragement and compassion that friends from Virginia bestow on Mom. Community and friendships are a blessing and these kind individuals will always have a special place in my heart.

In early 2022 my journal entries reflected Dad's declining condition and signs that Mom's health would become an issue:

1/11/2022 – In VA at Mom and Dad's. Dad was having a bad day. Had hit his head and said his kidneys were bad. I notice that Dad is really slipping. Praying for Your mercy and peace.

2/6/2022 – Tired and depressed last night. Mom not feeling well (kidney stone) and Dad is usually "down." The "what ifs" and feelings/thoughts of being overwhelmed flooded in. I can't foresee a good ending but it will be much worse if Mom has issues first; she is taking care of everything down there. Trusting You Lord. I am lost without You.

2/7/2022 – Feeling a little "blah" this morning. Part of it is Mom not feeling well and Dad continuing to go downhill. No matter what, You are faithful. A good Christian friend told me that "I need to write my own script" based on advice she once received. While I appreciate the sentiment, I can't write my own script. My parents are writing it for me. In reality, You have always written my script and I'm grateful because I would just mess things up on my own. Please give me strength, wisdom, and peace.

In February of 2022 I made a trip down to Mom and Dad's when their precious dog, Gretel, whom Dad especially loved dearly, began to have health issues. Mom said that the dog was sleeping a lot and appeared to be in pain. When I pulled up at the house Dad walked out and was holding his chest and walking erratically. He was understandably upset and anxious over the dog and I believed was having a heart attack. I tried consoling him but to no avail. These days he tended to seriously overreact to even the simplest issues. I took Gretel to an emergency veterinarian appointment where she was prescribed a new medicine. It seemed like the condition was not serious and that the dog would be fine but, unfortunately, time would reveal that she had bigger problems than were originally diagnosed. Sadly, those issues would soon lead to Gretel's demise.

Dad was getting progressively worse, evident by daily "incidents." On one visit he told me that he was locked out of his car. I checked things out and there was nothing wrong with his vehicle. He was also losing items such as his wallet, car keys, and money. He misplaced things and subsequently panicked when he couldn't remember where they were. Another time he could not get one of his combination safes to lock. I offered to help, surmising that a battery needed to be replaced. Dad got upset with me and protested, "No, it will never work!" I coaxed him into letting me try and, sure enough, I got the lock working again.

Back home one Saturday morning, I was on my way to the post office in my town when Mom called. As was usually the case, I knew this wasn't a "hello, how are you doing call." Evidently Dad had finished pumping gas at the local convenience store when he locked his keys in the car. He could not move the vehicle and the owner of the station became impatient when customers could not access the pump. I asked Mom where his spare keys were. I learned that the spare set was locked in a closet in Dad's office. Logically, my next question was, "Where are the keys to Dad's closet?" You probably correctly guessed that the closet key was on his keyring, locked in his vehicle.

It was always frustrating for me, being five hours away, when I could not provide hands-on help to my parents. Mom asked me to call their sheriff but I wanted to exercise another option first before burdening law enforcement with this issue: I called the local Ford dealership to see if they could open the vehicle remotely. The service manager knew Dad but told me that the vehicle was purchased in Lynchburg, and I would need to contact that dealership. The manager had to stay at the shop until noon but offered to pick Dad up when his shift ended. This is another testament to the kind people in the area; they look out for each other. I tried calling the dealership where Dad had purchased the car but, of course, it was Saturday, and the service department was closed. Finally, Mom called the sheriff who was able to get the vehicle unlocked. This was so unlike Dad, and yet another example of his cognitive decline.

In March of 2022 I made an "emergency" trip to my parents' after receiving a call from Dad. Mom had an episode with back pain and would end up in the Emergency Room (again).

My journal entry from 3/15/2022 says this:

At Mom and Dad's. I feel like calling "Mayday" or "Uncle." Mom was in the ER Sunday night. Still in excruciating pain. Can hardly move, can't walk. Back/leg pain. Dad was doing pretty well caring for her but now his leg and back are hurting. Praying for healing. Praying we can get a nurse or home health care worker in. I was supposed to go home today but not sure I can even leave tomorrow.

To this day, Mom has no recollection of me being there on this visit. I helped take her to the bathroom and provided for her personal needs because she had difficulty standing and walking. Dad was having back and leg pain so couldn't be much help with Mom.

This event, unbeknownst to me at the time, was a harbinger of what was to come in early 2023. I'm not sure if this injury was a continuation of a previous fall in the pasture or if something else contributed. Between this and developing neuropathy in her feet, she was in a great deal of pain and could do very little.

Thank God, we were able to obtain in-home Physical Therapy (PT) which helped with her pain and mobility, at least for the moment. Dad's issues were difficult enough and would worsen. Adding Mom to the mix would actually make the circumstances unbearable.

Throughout this storm it seemed that there was never a dull moment. Overnight on that same visit, Dad tripped getting out of bed and the loud noise from his fall woke me from a deep sleep. Whenever I visited, I would sleep in the back bedroom which was on the opposite side of the house. At first, the "thud" I heard didn't seem real and I thought that I was dreaming. But the noise was so loud that I actually thought someone had broken into the house. When I realized that something bad had actually happened, I rushed across the house into my parents' bedroom. Dad was standing there, bewildered and confused. I said, "Dad, are you okay?"

He replied, "No."

Me: "Did you fall?"

Dad: "Yes."

Me: "Did you hit your head?"

Dad: "I think so…"

Me: "Let me take you to the hospital."

Dad: "No, go back to bed."

I pleaded but could not force Dad to seek medical help. How could I sleep after that excitement in the middle of the night?

After the fall, my heart was racing. I lay awake thinking that Dad would likely die in his sleep. With his history of strokes and a severe fall like that, a brain bleed or some other complication was possible if not likely. While lying in bed, I prayed, and God gave me an indescribable peace. I selfishly thought, maybe this is for the best; it's a peaceful way for Dad to go and he's not in any pain. If I wake up and Dad is still with us, it's a miraculous blessing.

Dad's office was part of an addition to the house, accessible through the back bedroom (where I slept during visits) or via an outside door. I never cared for the design of the addition because the sole indoor access was through a bedroom, which wasn't an issue unless there were visitors. Dad had not slept well over the past several years so his routine was to get up at three or four in the morning and go down to his office.

When I stayed overnight, he would take a flashlight, walk out the front door and enter his office from the outside. Whenever he entered the office, he turned the light on, which was visible from the bedroom where I slept. He would sit at the window with his cat (appropriately named "White Cat" due to his predominant color). Before he started to decline, Dad would read, pay bills, and make plans in his office. These days he often just sat and stared out the window. Typically, on my visits, when I slept in the back bedroom, I would wait to see the light to his office go on. When that happened, I had a peace that Dad was alive for another day and that things would be okay.

The morning after his fall I waited for the office light to come on, but it never did. It was five a.m. and I assumed the worst. I walked out towards the living room, intending to find Dad in his bedroom. As I entered the dark living room, there he was in his chair. He appeared to be okay, save a big contusion on his arm and pain in his back. I thanked the Lord for sparing him.

Mom had improved somewhat physically after her ER visit and PT but cognitively she was showing some issues with sharpness. I also noticed that she was repeating herself occasionally. With her physical issues, specifically with the neuropathy, she could no longer drive a car. It had also become difficult for her to care for the farm animals.

Ultimately, she would need to pay someone to do it, although finding reliable, consistent help in their rural area had proven extremely challenging in the past.

At the conclusion of that eventful visit, I left for home after supervising a large delivery of hay to their barn. I felt badly leaving. Who would take care of the animals and cut the twenty-plus acres of grass when I'm not there? I prayed that somehow Mom and Dad would be okay when I went home. I again questioned why they lingered so long on that property with the many responsibilities and issues. But change is difficult. I can't judge too harshly because I don't know what I'll be like if I'm blessed to live into my eighties.

I was so consumed with Mom and Dad's health that I didn't stop and thank God for how He was sustaining and holding onto me. It's so easy to focus on our trials that we can become distracted and miss the fact that the Lord is good and in control. At least that's been true for me. I have to remind myself daily of the precious truth from Isaiah 26:3: "You will keep in perfect peace those whose minds are steadfast, because they trust in you." And He has kept me in His perfect peace through everything. He has never failed and never will. But I am not the smartest pupil, and the Lord continues to draw me closer to Him and teach me things I need to grow in my faith.

Dad had a good friend, Norman, who performed tasks such as repairing pasture fence, doors, and any other odd jobs Dad needed to be done. Norman was and is the consummate handyman. And Norman loved and admired my father. Even though he had other jobs, at this time Norman stepped up and agreed to cut the grass and feed the farm animals whenever I could not be there. I consider this a miracle and another example of God meeting our needs, given how difficult it was for my parents to find reliable help there. This lifted a big burden from my mind since Dad and Mom could no longer handle these tasks consistently. Philippians 4:19 says, "And my God will meet all your needs according to the riches of his glory in Christ Jesus." There is not a promise in His Word that He hasn't kept. I wouldn't be sitting here, telling this story, if not for Him.

Norman also came to the rescue as my parents' health deteriorated further. I don't know what we would have done if not for him standing in the gap when I couldn't be on site. He still keeps in touch with Mom and me to this day. Thank God for Norman who I consider a great friend myself.

My journal entry from 3/19/2022 says this:

_____

Assuming I'm still around, things will get hard. My parents' health, all of their "stuff," and their wishes. This last trip taught me that my strength is solely in You and that's where my eyes need to be fixed. I can only do what You've called me to do. Please have Your way.

_____

The Lord continued to answer my prayers. Mom called and said her doctor was sending a home nurse to evaluate her. I thanked God for providing and prayed about the future. I didn't sign up for all of this but was reminded that I made myself available to God when I left my career. It was becoming difficult, but I declared that I was open and willing to do whatever the Lord called me to do. Little did I know just how difficult things would become. I prayed that the Lord would continue to make things clear. God has done too much in my life for me not to believe and trust Him, too much that I can't otherwise explain. Too many blessings that I don't deserve.

Chapter 6: The Hits Keep Coming

The Lord is my strength and my shield; my heart trusts in Him, and He helps me. My heart leaps for joy, and with my song I praise Him.

Psalm 28:7

In late March of 2022, I was enjoying a nice quiet evening in my rec room with Diane when the phone rang. The caller ID indicated that the call originated from an unknown number in my parents' area code. Normally I don't answer our home phone from unknown numbers; nine times out of ten it's a Spam call. But I had a mini panic attack when I noticed the area code. These days, with Dad's unpredictable behavior, I expected the worst. Did something happen to Mom or Dad? This can't be good…

I picked up the phone and the woman identified herself as Dad's neighbor. I had never met her, nor did I know her. I quickly learned that she was the one who bought the house my late grandparents lived in. Dad and Mom had that house built back in the mid-1990s, adjacent to their property, when my grandparents could no longer care for themselves in New Jersey. I praise God that my dear Nana and Pop lived out their final days next door to their daughter and son-in-law.

Dad's neighbor told me that she was calling out of concern for him. She had seen him a few days earlier at the bottom of his driveway, picking up mail from his mailbox. He would drive his SUV to the end of the driveway, exit the vehicle, and walk to the box which was directly next to a busy four-lane highway. I was always cautious myself whenever I visited and fetched the mail. Vehicles sped by at a good clip and I always waited until the coast was clear before opening the mailbox. Naturally it made me nervous whenever Dad was so close to the road, especially with his health conditions.

The neighbor indicated that Dad was propped up against his vehicle, in pain. She observed that Dad's breathing was labored. Eventually he stabilized and was able to drive back to the house. She was so affected by the incident that she obtained my phone number from Mom and consequently called me. Of course, Mom was not happy that a stranger was "in her business." Still, I was grateful for, albeit shaken by, the call. I was thankful that someone there was looking out for my parents.

In a way, I wasn't surprised by the call. Dad's back was hurting from the recent fall in his bedroom and his health was not good, physically or mentally. It had not fully hit me yet but the responsibilities for my parents' health and safety were about to increase—big time. I continually reminded myself that they should have moved closer to their family, probably when Dad had his second stroke. I never wanted to say "I told you this would happen" but it was inevitable. They say you can't put the toothpaste back in the tube, so I had to lean on the Lord for strength. This was way bigger than I could handle but I take comfort in Paul's words from 2 Corinthians 12:9: "My grace is sufficient for you, for My power is made perfect in weakness."

On the 26th of March I wrote this in my journal:

Lots of voices out there. I've been feeling sorry for myself, second guessing what I've been doing for my parents, worried about what others think. Some have suggested, "Why don't you push your parents towards assisted living, they can't live on their own." Or, "This is what we did with my Dad..." Finally, "Just move them," as if I could legally and morally do that. Everyone means well but they aren't in my shoes just like I'm not in theirs. This is my storm and it's not the same as anyone else's. Sure, if my parents were in skilled care or assisted living my life would be much easier. But that is not what they wanted and we are not at that point. These are my parents.

They are not patients or residents. They are my parents whom I promised to protect. I have to do what is right for them.

I believe that God had arranged my life at this time to help my parents and allow them to live where they wanted, unless/until they got to the point where they couldn't care for themselves. Dad let me know that I was doing all the right things for them, and I reflected on his words often for comfort. I prayed, "Lord, You know my heart. You have blessed us beyond belief and my sole goal in helping my parents is to make their remaining years as safe and happy as possible, bringing glory to You. I don't want or need anything else. And above all I pray that their trust is in You, to spend eternity with You. Lord, please give me wisdom when I am personally attacked or misunderstood."

I visited my parents at the end of March and did some odd jobs around the house for them. Mom's physical condition improved somewhat but I noticed that she was becoming more forgetful, especially with her short-term memory. Dad still struggled and continued to gradually decline, but I was grateful for the good moments. I always tried to take away at least one positive memory from each visit.

On my birthday, Dad gave me a lovely card which he had handpicked. He asked me to sit down and read it out loud. He told me that every word in the card described me. The words were so sweet and encouraging; I couldn't make it through reading it when I started to cry. Dad was still "in there" and his heart was very tender. I am so undeserving of the kind words but grateful for the love Dad and Mom showed me that day. Looking back at moments like these gives me peace and gratitude, especially given where things stand now.

Sadly, their dog Gretel had to be put to sleep. After several emergency vet appointments where we thought things were improving, she struggled to walk and was in a great deal of pain. Heretofore undiagnosed, she had cancer throughout her back. It was very sad, and I worried that this might push Dad over the edge. Dad and Mom cared for a number of dogs and cats in Virginia over the years. Each time one passed away it was difficult. Gretel was a great dog for Mom and Dad. With everything happening there, this one was especially hard.

Mom and Dad were devastated and I asked them to wait and think hard before they introduce another dog to the household. They already had two cats and the care of a dog was one more thing they didn't need to worry about. But Mom told me that Dad wanted to get another dog right away. In spite of my feelings, I was empathetic and wanted them to be as happy as possible. To that end, I respectfully asked them to wait a few days until I could visit, and I would help them find a small dog at a shelter, emphasis on small.

I need to pause and tell you that my parents have not always been the most patient people. The word "impulsive" comes to mind. Over the years they have made hasty decisions when it comes to purchases and taking on responsibilities. The Bible tells us to "count the cost" and that counsel has not always been practiced by my parents (Luke 14:28). Sure enough, the following day, Mom sent me a text and said that they had adopted a new dog from the shelter. I asked, "Is it a small dog?" She said "yes."

I am not from Missouri but thought to myself, "Okay, show me!"[2] I hopped on the shelter's social media page and there was a picture of Mom and Dad with what looked like a hunting dog. This was not a small canine; it was a large hound! He had a cute face, and I appreciate my parents' hearts, but this was not the right dog for them. I tried to be supportive, but what were they thinking? They couldn't wait one more day until I visited?

I love dogs and "Buddy" was friendly enough, but way too big and extremely active for my parents to manage. My parents were also unaware when they adopted him, that Buddy is blind. I assume that the shelter didn't disclose that piece of information. When I went to visit my parents, I noticed that the dog would bump into things around the house and a subsequent vet appointment confirmed my layman's diagnosis. I later learned that Buddy had been in the shelter for a year and his siblings had all been adopted months before. Hmm. That should have been a red flag.

Buddy is a hunting dog by nature and was therefore too aggressive around their cat, Cricket, so was relegated to a screened-in porch in the front of the house. It was an

---

[2] Missouri has long been known as the "Show Me State." (www.brittanica.com/story/why-is-missouri-called-the-show-me-state)

extremely inconvenient situation. Mom had to leash the dog in order to get him through the house to the backyard where he could do his business. He also periodically used the porch as a bathroom which made the room unusable. Buddy always gave Mom (and me) a hard time when he had to go out. It was a fight to get the leash on and coax him from out of the porch area. I had trouble controlling the dog when I took him through the house to go outside. I am not a weak man, but it was all I could do to keep my balance when he yanked on his leash. I learned later that the dog had pulled Mom down several times. Unfortunately, this likely also contributed significantly to her back issues which would worsen in the near future.

Here is a journal entry from late May:

Talked to Mom yesterday. Depressed and said Dad is, too. She wondered aloud if she wants to stay there. Now was not a good time to move due to housing market. I wish that she had said this five or six years ago. Praying for wisdom and strength with my parents. She is "down;" wants things like a vacation that are not possible because of their life choices. Care of the animals tied them down. If they would have moved six years ago, things might be different.

The hits did keep coming. I showed up for a visit at the end of May and Dad was very upset. I tried to learn what was bothering him, but he kept repeating, "I did something I shouldn't have, I'm so stupid…" I finally had to ask: "Dad, what can be so bad? Did you hurt someone, were you hurt? What is it?" He replied, "I can't tell you, it's too bad, I'm so stupid…"

First of all, Dad was not stupid. He is one of the smartest people I've ever known. I have no idea what was going through his mind, but this terrible disease robbed him of large parts of his memory and his emotions. When something went wrong, he would default to self-deprecation. These days he would say, "I'm sorry" quite a bit. I had to remind him that there was nothing to be sorry about. It's been so difficult to watch. But he is still my Dad, he commands my respect, and he is not stupid!

I found that when Dad obsessed over something, it was best to ask a few questions and then just leave it alone. Eventually he would tell me or forget about it. That afternoon, I was going out to feed the farm animals and Dad was in his favorite living room chair. I noticed that he was holding a receipt and a loyalty card from the grocery store he frequented in the nearest town. I surmised that something happened at the store. Dad asked me, "Where are you going?" "To feed the animals," I replied. Dad asked, "Where is Mom?" I said, "In the bedroom I think, do you want me to get her?" He replied in the affirmative. After I told Mom that Dad wanted to see her, I started to walk out the front door and Dad said, "You'd better stay, too." I knew that he was ready to spill the beans.

As it turned out, he had gone to the grocery store first thing that morning, placed several items into his cart, and went to the checkout register. He fished around in his pocket and wallet and could not find his credit card. Dad knew most of the employees at the store, so they took pity and combed the aisles in search of Dad's lost card. But to no avail. Finally, a manager approached Dad and said, "Don't worry about it, your bill is taken care of."

As Dad told the story and I pieced things together I summarized: "So, you couldn't find your card and the store paid your bill? Dad, that's not a bad thing." Thinking he had run up a large grocery bill I asked, "What was the total for the groceries?" He replied sheepishly, "Twenty dollars." I told Dad that, in the first place, that is not a lot of money. Secondly, and most importantly, the manager's action was a testimony to how much they thought of my dad. "Dad, they care about you and paid it forward. You've always taught me to be generous. The next time you go into the store give the manager forty or fifty dollars and tell him to pay a grocery bill for someone who is less fortunate."

It took a while, but Dad finally came to terms with this. He eventually found his credit card, in the driveway where his vehicle was parked. But it was another sign of forgetfulness as he continually misplaced important items. It was also a sign of Dad overreacting to the slightest issues and blaming himself.

I left that visit, grateful to have spent precious time with Dad and Mom. However, I had an ongoing, overwhelming concern about what would happen if my parents could no longer care for themselves. While we had our good moments, Dad had gotten progressively worse with depression, moodiness, confusion, and expression. He was in a doctor's care, but I wasn't sure if the medicines were helping him. I confessed to the Lord that I didn't know what to do other than tread water. The reality is, Mom and Dad should be in a downsized, less-complicated, no-animals/farm situation. The property and "stuff" would be too much for me to manage, let alone two people in their eighties in less-than-ideal health. I was trusting God for strength and wisdom.

On a visit in mid-July, I noticed that Dad was very confused. His friend Norman, who helped around the farm and spent lots of time with Dad, told me that Dad was slipping mentally. Dad would often use these common phrases which continued into 2023: "I don't know what I'm doing, I don't know where I am, I don't know what to do next."

Truthfully, I didn't know what to do next either. I was grateful that I had the opportunity to share the Gospel with Mom and Dad before I left for home on that visit. I had shared it years ago and they said they had received Christ. But I needed to be sure and didn't want to pass up an opportunity. I prayed that their confession was genuine and I trust God at His Word. I cannot save them or anyone else, only the Lord Jesus Christ can.

In late July I was sitting in my Sunday School class when I received a text from Mom. With the evolving events in Virginia my antenna always went up when Mom texted; seldom was the news good. The crisis du jour was that Dad had lost his wallet. I was five hours away so could not offer any tangible assistance, but I did pray. Diane had smartly placed sensors on common items my parents used, such as Dad's wallet, Mom's cell phone, and Dad's car keys. The sensors worked with a remote control which would help locate these items in the event that they went missing. I suggested via text that Mom use the "beeper" to find Dad's wallet. Hours passed and Dad was freaking out. The wallet could not be found, even with the beeper. I prayed that God would help them find the item. After hours of searching Mom found it in high grass on the twenty-acre property, near a shed. How the wallet ended up there is anyone's guess but I thanked the Lord for answered prayer.

Dad's mind was deteriorating. I prayed that the Lord would protect him and Mom, and help me to discern when hard decisions would need to be made. Those days were just around the corner…

Chapter 7: A Divine Encounter

Taste and see that the Lord is good; blessed is the one who takes refuge in Him.

Psalm 34:8

I t had been a tough couple of years. We needed a vacation. I needed a vacation. After making numerous trips to Virginia to care for my parents, I craved a break and some time away. Anywhere! I suggested to Diane that we take a short trip to the Jersey Shore. Frankly, I didn't care where we went as long as we got away. Of course, I was concerned about going too far in the event that things went sideways in Virginia. I talked to Mom and Dad before we planned anything and got assurance that they would not take any unnecessary risks and minimize the chance of any "incidents."

The last thing I wanted was to be more than five hours away in an emergency. Obviously, with their health and Dad's unpredictable behavior, I took their "assurance" with a grain of salt. But Dad, even in his declining state, wanted us to have a vacation. He was always more concerned about my well-being than his own.

While I looked forward to getting away, an annoying stye had developed on my right eyelid. It had grown to the point where it was large, ugly, and impairing my vision. A few days before we were to leave on the trip, the stye had become painful and I was miserable. Diane suggested that we cancel the trip because my eye was giving me so much trouble. I protested and insisted we go; I really needed to get away and clear my mind. I'd find a way to live with the stye, but it certainly was a huge annoyance.

I grew up about an hour west of Atlantic City. When I was younger, we would visit Wildwood, Ocean City, and beaches in the southern part of New Jersey. I wanted something a little different, so our vacation this year would take us to several central Jersey beaches, including Belmar, Spring Lake, Sea Girt and Asbury Park. When we were first married, we lived close to these beach towns, and I looked forward to checking them out. The trip really did provide the spiritual balm we both needed, and we enjoyed a few days of fun in the sun, good food, and relaxation. I checked in with my parents daily and things were stable, thank God.

The night before we planned to head home from the shore, I was sitting in the hotel room, when an idea came to me. Looking back, I have no doubt that the Lord planted the thought in my mind. I've learned to never ignore that still, small voice. Often, it's the subtle things God uses to bring blessings to His people and glory to His Name. I said to Diane, "Let's not rush home tomorrow. Instead of taking the usual (shortest) route home, why don't we ride down the coast, walk the boardwalk in Seaside Heights, and then head to south Jersey for lunch at a restaurant we like? Then we'll go through Philly and take the long way home." Diane agreed to the plan.

Early that Wednesday morning we enjoyed a beautiful ride down the coast and stopped in Seaside Heights. We spent about an hour walking the boardwalk. My goal was then to make our way to route 70 West and head towards Philadelphia for lunch.

We hadn't quite made it to route 70 when I felt my cell phone vibrate. My cousin Kathy had sent me a text message through social media. Since I was driving, I asked Diane to read the message. Kathy's message read, "Can you send me your phone number? I need to talk to you right away."

I love my cousins but we don't have much contact due to distance. I had not seen them in a number of years. Therefore, I sensed that this message was not good news. Just for background, my cousins Kathy, Barbara, and Bonnie are daughters to Martha, my favorite aunt. Aunt Martha at the time was Dad's only living sibling, and they spoke on the phone regularly. The calls always lifted Dad's spirits. Coincidentally, Dad had not heard from Aunt Martha in several months, which was unusual. This made me further suspect that something was going on with her health.

Diane sent Kathy my number and the phone rang almost immediately. I picked up on speaker phone and Kathy gave me some sad news: her mother, my last living aunt, was gravely ill and under hospice care. Aunt Martha was "in and out" of consciousness but asked Kathy to contact me. Aunt Martha wanted me to break the news about her condition to Dad. My aunt knew of Dad's situation and health, and did not want to upset him. Frankly, I didn't know how I would tell Dad without upsetting him.

Kathy provided some details about her mom's illness but said that she was at peace and not suffering. I was grateful for that. She had lost her husband, my favorite Uncle Howard, a number of years ago, and was ready to join him in heaven. Dad and my uncle were very close, and Dad took it hard when Uncle Howard died. The family also lost my cousin, Hucky, years ago at a much-too-young age.

I asked Kathy if my aunt was at home and she informed me that her mom was at Bonnie's house, confined to a hospital bed. I knew exactly where Aunt Martha lived because I visited the house growing up and even a few times as an adult. However, I did not know where any of my cousins were living now. I did know that they were all somewhere in south Jersey but I had no idea which towns.

Since we were in New Jersey and headed towards Philly I asked Kathy, "Do you think I could see your mom one last time? I would love to visit her." Kathy replied, "Let me text Bonnie and ask her." Bonnie responded to Kathy and said that the timing wasn't good; her mom was asleep and not up to visitors. I was disappointed but certainly understood the situation. I told Kathy that I would be praying for all of them.

Kathy also reminded me that the memorial service for Aunt Martha was already planned and that she wanted me there to sing a song about Heaven, written by Alan Jackson. Several years ago, Aunt Martha spoke to Dad and asked him to ask me if I would sing the song at her funeral. Dad wrote the name of the song on an index card which I had displayed on my desk for several years. I think I listened to the song once or twice, but I wasn't familiar enough with it to play and sing it live. Based on this phone call I would start learning the song and was honored to fulfill my aunt's wishes.

Before I could hang up, Kathy said, "Wait, Bonnie texted and said that Mom woke up and would really like to see you!" I asked for Bonnie's address since I had no idea where she lived. I praised God when Kathy gave me the address. Miraculously we would be heading right through that area on our way to Philly! What are the chances that we were in that spot, at that moment in time? This was not the normal route I should have taken home and there were several reasons why we shouldn't be on this trip (namely my ugly, painful stye). I'd seen enough of these "coincidences" in my life to know that only God could have orchestrated this perfect timing. I believe that He placed the plan to take this route in my thoughts the night before.

A few years ago, I had the privilege of seeing my Uncle Joe, Dad's older brother, right before he went home to be with the Lord. The circumstances at that time were God-inspired as well. I was honored and blessed that God was now giving me the same opportunity to visit and pray with Aunt Martha before she went "home."

When Diane and I arrived at Bonnie's house, we were greeted by her, her husband, and my cousin Barbara. It was great to see my cousins after all of these years. After we spoke for a few minutes, Bonnie took us in to see Aunt Martha. I hardly recognized her when I walked into the room. She was frail but still beautiful, almost glowing. Her smile and disposition told me that she was at peace. In the bed next to her was a picture of my late Uncle Howard, decked out in his military uniform. He was a great man with a wonderful sense of humor and positive outlook of life. He was such an inspiration, always upbeat and positive. I remember him well and miss his laughter and smile.

Aunt Martha spoke in a whisper and first took my hand and asked, "Rob, would you pray for me?" I held her hand, tears streaming down my face, and lifted her up to the Lord. More tears flowed when she told me how much I meant to her. It was such a beautiful moment, and I was in awe of God who arranged this holy meeting.

Distance kept us apart through the years, but we were continually on each other's minds. She was one of my biggest cheerleaders behind the scenes. I have a card of encouragement that she wrote me when I was in Texas back in the 80s, telling me that she heard that I "met a girl" there. That girl was my wife, Diane. Additionally, when I wrote my second book, *Family Love Letters,* Dad sent my aunt a copy of the book. She called me during one of my visits to Mom and Dad's to tell me how much she loved it, and that she was passing it on to my cousins. She went out of her way to sincerely encourage me, and it meant so much!

As she lay there in the hospital bed we reminisced about the past and wonderful memories we shared. She confidently declared that she was ready to see Jesus which is really all that matters in this life. Her faith and peace in the face of death was inspiring and wonderful. It strengthened my hope for an eternity with my Savior. She continually apologized about not telling Dad of her condition. She was so concerned about him, her only living sibling. I sympathized with her concern based on what Dad was going through with his health issues. She asked that I break the news gently and take good care of her brother. I promised that I would, further confirmation from God that I needed to be doing what I was doing for my parents.

Aunt Martha repeated what Kathy had told me: her private service had already been carefully planned. She asked if I would be there to sing the song she had selected. She sweetly said, "I'll understand if you can't come." There was no way I was going to miss her service. As I said earlier, Dad had given me the name of the song a few years ago. I promised to have it ready so that I could sing it with guitar accompaniment. She made it very clear that she only wanted immediate family at her graveside service and gave strict instructions not to tell anyone else. She had everything well-planned and did not want any attention or fanfare. I did not question her and was impressed by her humility and grace. I honored her request.

Once again, I was amazed at how God made this encounter possible. There was nothing Christian about me nor my relationships growing up. I was so far from the Lord. Moreover, we never talked about God or religion as a family. Yet here I was praying with my aunt all these years later. And before I left, I then had the opportunity to pray with my cousins, in a circle with hands joined. In the midst of sorrow, God gave us peace, joy and fellowship. I thank God for Aunt Martha's faith, support of me over the years, and the gift of seeing her before her death.

I wasn't sure how I would break the news to Dad so I took the easy way out: I called Mom and left her a message. I thought the news might be better coming from her. Mom found the opportunity to tell Dad about his sister and later told me that he actually handled the news pretty well.

Aunt Martha lived a few more weeks before going home to be with Jesus. I had hoped to be at home when it happened so that Mom could let Dad know. To be honest, I wanted to avoid seeing Dad get upset. But providentially, I was with Dad and Mom in Virginia when Kathy sent me the news via text message. I prayed and waited a while before taking Dad aside to let him know that his sister was now with the Lord. He handled it as well as could be expected and I thank God that he didn't go over the edge. I believe that God had a reason for me being there with him at that time. I continue to be amazed and blessed by how He creates circumstances which not only fulfill His purposes but also bring blessings to His people. All glory to Him!

Diane and I were honored to attend the small homecoming service for Aunt Martha in south Jersey, in the cemetery where my uncle and grandmother are buried. It was a warm, breezy, beautiful morning where the service was held. A pastor paid honor to Aunt Martha and delivered a short message about our hope in Christ, His love and sacrifice for us, and our inheritance in heaven when we belong to Him. I was then blessed to sing the song of faith in her honor and to spend time with my cousins and their families. Well-done, Aunt Martha.

For me this encounter was like a rainbow in the midst of the storm. Was the timing of our vacation trip a coincidence? Did the route I took that morning happen by accident? Was this a miraculous, divinely appointed encounter from God? Decide for yourself but I have no doubt.

Chapter 8: Things Begin to Fall Apart

Trust in the Lord with all your heart and lean not on your own understanding; in all your ways submit to Him, and He will make your paths straight.

Proverbs 3:5-6

It was now September of 2022 and Dad's decline continued rapidly. He hardly drove and, when he did, it was for very short distances. He often became confused about starting and turning off his vehicle. His SUV had all kinds of issues which the repair shop could never resolve. He continually mentioned that he wanted to purchase a new pickup truck to use around his property. Mom didn't think it was practical because of the cost and Dad's condition. I agreed with her that it wasn't the best idea nor timing, but Dad had the funds and had worked hard all his life. It was something he really wanted. If the truck would give him some joy, why not?

I wish I had been there when he and Mom went shopping at a dealership about thirty miles from his home. I assumed that Dad would choose a practical small truck, but he opted for one that was way too large for his needs, in my opinion. I don't know if this was his dream vehicle or if the salesman "sold" Dad on it. Regardless, while he was able to drive it home, he hardly used it after that because the technology was so complicated. With his cognition and decline, he became afraid to drive the new vehicle. Most of the time the truck sat in the driveway and Dad used the smaller Subaru to get around. As it turned out, the Subaru developed battery issues, and we would eventually need the truck to transport Mom and Dad around to appointments and errands. When people learned that Dad was no longer driving the truck, it became very attractive; several people expressed a desire for the vehicle which was disheartening to me. With everything going on the last thing on my mind was my parents' "stuff." Their health and well-being were my priority.

It became difficult for me to focus on anything other than what was happening in Virginia. When I was at home I continually thought of my parents. The situation there was like a ticking time bomb. Little did I know that things were about to explode.

On September 10, 2022, I was waiting for my usual morning text from Mom. I texted a few times and didn't receive a response. I knew that she had a doctor's appointment, but it was unusual for her not to respond in a timely manner, even if to simply state, "We're okay." After several hours passed, I contacted my younger brother who had also been unsuccessful reaching my parents. By noon I was panicking; my parents live in a very rural area, isolated from any close neighbors. If something bad happened, I would have no easy way of knowing.

I hated to be alarmed but I finally called the county sheriff's office which sent an officer to the property for a welfare check. I need to state that in this instance and events to come, the sheriff's office in Virginia was amazing; supportive, friendly, responsive, compassionate, and empathetic. The county is very large and spread out, but Dad was a friend to law enforcement, so they knew who he was and looked out for him. I cannot say enough about my respect and gratitude for the sheriff's office and first responders. Before long I would get to know several of them very well.

The sheriff's office is about fourteen miles from my parent's place, so it took a little while until I received a call back. A law enforcement officer checked out the property and said that the house was secure. My Dad's pickup truck was parked out front and the Subaru was not there, which meant to me that my parents were not at the house. The sheriff ran the license plate and said that he would be on the lookout for my parents' car.

You can't make this stuff up: while I was on the phone with the sheriff Mom texted me, like nothing had happened.

She told me that she had a long doctor's visit and there was no phone reception at the office. She then went to Physical Therapy for her foot. She and Dad ended their trip with a visit to the grocery store. She apologized for forgetting to text, but I was upset. I reminded her how critical it was for her to stay in touch every day. Until I heard from her, I had no idea if my parents were okay.

The silver lining to this event was that I established myself as an emergency contact with the sheriff's office. This way I would be contacted right away if my parents had any type of crisis. I believe that this was another way the Lord was working in this situation because of what was about to unfold.

I wrote this in my journal on 9/18/2022:

_____

Woke up about 1 this morning and sensed You speaking to me. I've been struggling with headaches, chest pain, stomach pain, fatigue, and I'm sure that stress plays no small role. I feel that You reinforced these Biblical truths to me:

1. You are in control. I have little control. I need to remember and accept that You have a purpose.
2. This world is not my home. I am just a pilgrim here.
3. I can't love the things of this world. It's about loving You and people.
4. I shouldn't worry but always pray (Phil 4)

I have peace with what You spoke to me. Please keep me filled with Your Spirit and keep my eyes fixed on You.

In late September I visited Mom and Dad again. Dad's behavior and emotional state were more "down" than "up." He was on anxiety meds, but I wasn't sure how effective they were. His doctor, who I greatly respect, was trying different things to stabilize Dad. It is clear to me now that he needed more specialized care, but it wasn't available where he lived. He struggled physically and was depressed. I was grateful that he was consuming a few meals but most times he refused to eat. I learned later that he was "nourishing" himself with snacks and sweets which he kept hidden in his office.

We did have a few laughs, but the visit was stressful. Things got to the point where I began to dread each visit. The trips were getting more difficult, and Dad was very unpredictable. I prayed for Mom who had her own issues and took the brunt of Dad's behavior and moods.

In early October, I agreed to visit Mom and Dad for four days, at Mom's request. Each of them had doctor appointments and Dad was really afraid to drive, probably a good thing in terms of safety. I know it may not sound "Christian," but I was not looking forward to being there for that length of time. I prayed often for strength because I was stressed and becoming exhausted with the long drive and the uncertainty of Dad's health.

I drove Dad to the hospital for a brain MRI. Afterwards, he was in pain with a severe headache. He was also very emotional after the procedure. I didn't know what to do to comfort him. Thankfully he felt better the following day. This was getting to be like a roller coaster ride, up and down. The brain MRI showed damage from previous strokes but nothing new, according to his doctor. I continued to suspect that Dad had some form of a cognitive disease, but no doctor would specifically diagnose it.

I also took Mom to an orthopedist in Lynchburg, an hour-and-a-half drive, for a consultation. Based on x-rays and MRIs the doctor diagnosed her with several spinal/back issues which were causing her pain. I never dreamed how this diagnosis would snowball in 2023 and affect her life (and ours) to this day. If it were just Dad…

At the end of October, Mom called me and said that Dad didn't want to live anymore. He had become extremely paranoid. He called me, in a panic, complaining that Mom was conspiring with a woman to "do something" with the property and their money. I couldn't imagine what this was all about, so I called Mom. She assured me that there was no one else in the house. Did Dad imagine this, or did he overhear Mom on the phone with someone? I never figured out what was troubling him that day. The doctor adjusted his anxiety medications, but it didn't seem to help; things were falling apart rapidly. I prayed for wisdom and strength and that the Lord would protect my parents from harm.

Some time later, Mom called and said she needed me to come down to their home right away. Dad had not been paying the bills, and she was concerned about a credit card statement which was coming due. When she tried to intervene, Dad pushed back and would not listen to her. I had previously set up online access to my parents' credit card account so I was able to monitor charges and payments. I also kept an eye out for any fraudulent activity to protect them. Dad had his own manual system where he paid the bill via an automated phone system. He kept a slip of paper, which listed the 800 number for the credit card company and his account number, next to the office phone. I didn't question Dad, but he had an unusual practice of paying a few dollars on the account every couple of days.

When I checked the account online, I noticed that Dad had not made a payment on the credit card bill in almost a month. This is what Mom had suspected and why she was concerned. The due date was approaching, and Dad would be hit with a large finance charge if payment wasn't made soon. This was so out of character for the financial expert I knew who was on top of everything related to bills and money. I mentioned the bill to Mom, and she paid it by telephone. That action sent Dad into a tizzy; he became belligerent and unreasonable. Mom pleaded with me to come down and intervene. I was about to make the first of many "emergency," five-hour trips to southern Virginia.

I wrote this in my journal on 10/31/2022, prior to leaving:

---

4 a.m. Monday. Good morning, Lord. Thank You for this gift of a new day. This could be one of the hardest days of my life—a difficult trip to my parents'. Dad is not well; mental and cognitive decline. He does not know I'm coming. Please give me supernatural strength and wisdom. Tired, headache, and chest pain all day yesterday. Can't do this on my own. I will give You the glory, in Jesus's Name.

Before I left, I was anxious, tired, and a little resentful. I felt like I was reaping the consequences of my parents', especially Mom's, decision to remain in Virginia too long. I admit that I had a chip on my shoulder when I arrived, close to 10 a.m. the morning of October 31st. Dad was "surprised" to see me. I should have been more empathetic, especially to Dad. It hadn't dawned on me yet that he had a brain disease, and it wasn't "him" deliberately behaving the way he was. Mom would sometimes lament, "How could your father do this to me?" The truth is, he couldn't help it. It wasn't "him." He had a disease.

When I walked into the house, Mom was smiling as if nothing had happened. I told my parents that I wanted to isolate myself in a bedroom, alone, for a few minutes, to gather my thoughts and come up with a plan going forward. I said that we would have a family meeting in the living room at 11 to discuss the future. Dad tersely said, "I'm not coming."

Years ago, I would have never said this to the man I respected so much, and often feared, but I sternly replied, "Oh yes you are!" Mom said, "You're going to make us move, aren't you?" She didn't realize that I couldn't force them to do anything, nor would I, but I kept my cards close to the vest and said, "Not if you cooperate with me. Things can't go on this way." Of course, her canned reply was, "We're fine!" I thought, "Really, then why am I here?"

I had no idea what to do in this worsening situation. I sat in the bedroom quietly and earnestly prayed to the Lord for wisdom. After being still for a while, I believe that God gave me the words to say and a plan to at least keep my parents safe in Virginia. Consequently, I jotted down some points I wanted to make and have my parents agree to. At 11 a.m. I brought a kitchen chair into the living room and sat across from Mom and Dad, facing them. I felt like a judge meting out a sentence.

I first laid out their current reality: They were not managing down there, they were not safe, and they needed help. Dad, and especially Mom, took pride in their self-sufficiency but things were out of control. As much as I love my parents, they chose to live there and I could only do so much due to the distance. I needed a lifeline and wanted them to "meet me halfway" so to speak. Mom often complains that she had no family there to help. To this day she'll sometimes tell people, "I couldn't get my son to move down to Virginia to take care of me." As much as I love my parents, relocating to Virginia was not a practical solution for this situation.

I reminded Mom and Dad that I was doing my best, given the distance and circumstances, to keep them safe! Their safety and health were my number one priority. I was continually worried about their well-being and these long trips, frequent and often on a moment's notice, were taking a toll on my physical and mental health.

The first "demand" I had was that they would hire someone, within a month, to care for the farm animals. Dad certainly could not do it, and Mom wasn't doing what was required; she had too many physical limitations to safely care for them. I was also concerned for her safety, being outside in the elements and alone in the pastures. I managed things when I was on-site but couldn't be there all the time.

Second, I insisted that they allow me to take over the responsibility of paying their bills. Dad was misplacing mail and not balancing his checkbook, and I did not want them to have any issues with unpaid bills. Lastly, I insisted that they let me set up part-time home health care so that someone could come in a few times a week and help them. Part-time care would give me some relief as well as peace of mind when I could not be there. Little did I realize that the need for full-time care would eventually become a reality. In the back of my mind, given the rural area where they lived, I wasn't certain if there was home health care available nor the extent of their services.

As Mom typically did and sometimes continues to do whenever the immediate crisis passes, she responded, "We're fine, we can handle things, I don't need help..." I said, "Mom, you're not fine. Look how you're living! Look how I'm living! And you begged me to drop everything and come here today. This is unsustainable and we need to make some changes!"

I said to Dad, "Do you agree with my proposal?" He reluctantly said, "I guess we don't have a choice..." "Mom?" She replied, "We don't need someone coming in to help us." I insisted, "If you don't agree, we'll need to take more drastic measures. You are not safe here by yourselves. And I cannot live here with you. You've put me in a difficult situation." Mom reluctantly agreed to the plan. So off I went to the bedroom to make some phone calls.

The first few calls were discouraging; I could not find a care agency which would service my parents' county. It's understandable based on where they lived. It was always a challenge to get people to come to the house for services due to the proximity of my parents' property to civilization. Lynchburg was the closest big city, approximately seventy minutes away, depending on which part of town you were going to. Richmond was a bit farther.

By God's provision and grace, after several unsuccessful phone calls, one agency said that they had a branch about thirty miles from my parents. They took my information and said they would get back to me; they needed to determine if someone from that office could handle my parents' case. Thankfully, I later received a call back that the agency would accept the case and send a Registered Nurse (RN) the following day to assess Dad. This was a miraculous answer to prayer! I decided to stay the night so that I could meet and talk to the nurse the following morning.

I was convinced that this was a miracle. Not only were we fortunate to hire this agency but the services they provided were exactly what Dad and Mom needed. They provided cooking and light housekeeping, which was a blessing. Mom was not cooking meals for herself (or Dad) and needed help around the house. The agency even provided transportation to stores and appointments which meant that I didn't have to worry about Dad driving. Importantly, they would also remind my parents when to take their medicines. Above all, when someone was scheduled to be there with my parents, I had peace knowing that they were being cared for. Companionship was no small factor in the services the agency provided. My parents did not have sufficient human interaction, in my opinion. I am not a doctor but cannot imagine that isolation is good for people with memory issues.

Mom did not want someone there all the time, but I got her to agree to two or three times a week. When we scheduled help, based on caregiver availability, the minimum visit was four hours. To be sure, elder care does not come cheap, but this care was affordable since it was part-time. The time would come, however, when they would need 24/7 care but that was nearly impossible to obtain. Still, looking back, we would have been lost without the timely care this agency provided.

The following day, the RN showed up to talk with Dad, Mom, and me. The nurse was a skilled, empathetic, compassionate, Christian woman. Even though the care was mainly for Dad, the nurse said that they would include Mom as well. "If we're cooking for Dad, we're cooking for Mom, too!" This was a blessing both financially and emotionally.

The nurse asked Dad a number of questions to assess his condition. He was engaged at first but quickly shut down. I remember him asking, "Are we about done here?" He was really struggling mentally, cognitively, and physically. We scheduled the first four hours of care for the following day, which would be a Friday. I planned to stay in a hotel on Thursday night, about twenty miles from Mom and Dad's place, and head home on Friday morning so I would not be there for the first day of care. I prayed that this would all work out.

While the agency provided the services I just mentioned, I was most grateful for the companionship they offered. The agency wanted the caregiver to become like family to my parents. That blessed me; Mom and Dad had a few friends but were isolated due to the rural nature of the area. I felt like the company and "someone to talk to" would really be good for both of them.

Mom continued to push back and said, "I can handle things, I don't need anyone here." I don't know if Mom's attitude was driven by cost of care, pride, or something else. But I get it; we all cherish our independence, and Mom is proud of her accomplishments and self-reliance. It's humbling when we have to ask for help. The reality is, we come into this world being totally dependent on someone else for our well-being and survival. In the latter seasons of life, we often also become dependent due to physical or other limitations. I feel bad for elders who have no one to look out for them.

I stood firm with Mom and said that she had to schedule the agency at least twice per week, even if it was for the minimum of four hours. The reality was that this assistance would benefit all of us. And as I said earlier, a time would soon come when she would become desperate for full-time care but, unfortunately, it was not available 24/7.

I felt badly that I was so adamant in my approach with Mom and Dad and may have scared them with the way I came across. But this was the only option short of moving or assisted living for Dad. I was surprised that Dad seemed open to moving and rehoming the animals. It would later become clear that Dad had been ready to move for the past few years. Mom, not so much.

I can't emphasize this enough: Although things would get much worse, obtaining this care at this time was crucial to my parents' survival, (and likely mine too)! Without it, things would have been unsustainable and both likely would have ended up in some type of assisted living, skilled care, or worse. I was getting burned out making the five-hour trips. Further, the level of care needed and managing the property and animals was more than I could adequately provide. It is also highly likely that something unexpected, such as a fatal fall, may have happened. I am forever grateful for the need this agency met.

Things got to the point where I became very discouraged. Mom still thought she could do it alone yet was at wits end because of Dad. She was not happy with having the help in her home, but she needed it. What gives me some solace is the fact that Dad, in his lucid moments, would have done what I was doing. Years ago, he set the standard when Mom's parents could no longer care for themselves. He did whatever it took to ensure their safety and well-being, regardless of others' opinions. Dad always took good care of Mom as well during those times when she was sick or recovering from surgeries.

During this visit I felt hardened and hurt because Dad's behavior reminded me of times growing up. It brought back painful memories of times when my childhood was not so happy. Time would reveal that his condition exacerbated his negative emotions. I was not sure what to do if this plan didn't work out. When I was younger, I depended on my parents to take care of me. Now the child had become the parent, and I was in uncharted waters.

I hate to admit it, but it got to a point where I could no longer stand being in their Virginia home. The atmosphere was so negative and stressful. I could not sleep and almost became physically sick. It is only by God's grace and care that I survived the situation. But I love my parents and only wanted what is best for them. I know that the Lord was there with me. He is good and would work all of this out for His glory. But it would get even more difficult, and quickly.

After the visit from the agency RN, I drove to the hotel and stayed the night. I left for home the following morning. I arrived at my house, relieved after the very stressful visit, when my younger brother called me in a panic. "Mom called and she is hysterical. She said she wants me (my brother) to get down there right away. I'm ready to pack a bag and head down but I've got to work. Should I go?" My heart sank; "I literally just walked in the door after driving for five hours," I replied, "Hang tight. Let me call down there and see what's going on. I hope I don't have to turn around and go back."

I was upset that Mom called my brother and not me, perhaps because of my approach on the emergency visit. It turned out that the new caregiver, on her first day, reminded Dad to eat and he had a fit. He told Mom he is selling the house and moving. I talked Mom off the ledge and things calmed down. The caregiver was actually wonderful with my parents, and I prayed that they didn't mess up these arrangements. Kaye, who became their primary caregiver, got Dad to talk about his career and the fact that she had a relative in the same line of work. Mom even texted me later and said, "Dad is engaging with Kaye." That was music to my ears! This care was my lifeline and, while the caregiver was only there for a few hours a week, I could feel at peace during the times when someone was present.

I worked in Information Technology (IT) for many years and would get unexpected calls at all hours and on weekends. I celebrated the day when I retired from that career, knowing that the calls would stop. Now I felt like I was back in those days again. This seemed like déjà vu all over. And the calls at all hours would increase with what was to come. Unexpected calls at any hour, while not as frequent, continue to this day.

Spiritually, I felt like I was falling apart. While I went through the motions of journaling and enjoying a quiet time of Bible reading and prayer, it became routine. I was distracted and it became difficult to focus. Still, I am thankful that I never missed my devotional time, up until then, but I felt like my walk with the Lord had become stagnant. I had taken an indefinite break from church activities, including worship leading and Sunday School teaching, two things I love to do. I simply wasn't around enough nor in the right frame of mind to give my best to those ministries. Ministry takes preparation and I insist on giving my best to the Lord. But I had little time due to the travel and circumstances in Virginia. Still, I know that God was holding me close.

My parents consumed my thoughts, and I second-guessed everything I did. Yes, they shouldn't be living on a huge property with farm animals in the middle of nowhere, in their eighties. Yes, I gently and later more sternly begged them to downsize and move, but Mom especially pushed back. All of that notwithstanding, I felt that the Lord called me to help them. Hopefully I've done that.

I had already made at least a dozen trips to Virginia, and it was only November. Sleeping at their house was beyond stressful, so I started staying overnight at the hotel which had become my "third home." Mom took it personally and let her displeasure with me be known to my brother and sister. The hotel stays were an expense for me, and I felt bad about not staying with my parents, but it was the only way I could sleep at night. I had not been taking care of myself and felt the effects physically, mentally, and spiritually. Looking back, I'm grateful that I survived but it was only by God's strength.

In early November, my brother visited my parents. I was always grateful when one of my siblings spent time with them. It gave me peace knowing that family was there with

Mom and Dad. My brother called and told me that Dad expressed resentment towards me, I assume because of my stern approach on the recent "Emergency" visit. I know that Dad would have done the same for his or Mom's parents in the past, but the words still hurt. Over time, God has taught me to ignore negative speech and complaints, but some days it gets to me, especially if I'm tired. Dad was not the same person I knew. Mom is not the same person I knew. It takes an intentional, daily effort to come to grips with that fact. I was and am grateful for the good moments we share together.

I didn't know what else to do. Looking back now, this was a moving train, and I was trying hard to stay on it. Managing their health, safety, finances, and to some extent, the care of their property and animals was overwhelming. I neglected responsibilities at home in favor of my parents' needs. My daughters were preparing for major life events that I wanted to be a part of but couldn't devote much attention to. We had a sick cat which required emergency vet visits and meds twice a day. Since Dad's second stroke in 2016 I'd fashioned my life around visiting my parents and making sure they could live safely in the home. My life seemed out-of-control.

I prayed that my parents would accept their situation and avail themselves of the caregiver's services. I prayed that they would see the blessing for what it was. When Mom complained to her family doctor about the cost of home health care and the fact that "she didn't need it," I was grateful that the doctor backed me up and reiterated what I had stressed to my parents: She confirmed that Mom and Dad needed the help and should be grateful that they were able to get it.

The caregiver kept me informed, calling me periodically with updates on Mom and Dad. One day she drove Mom to the library and Dad agreed to ride along. I was grateful that he wanted to get out. He had made the decision to no longer drive which was for the best. Instead, he rode his lawn tractor around the property. That may seem strange, but I didn't question him; that's what made him comfortable.

My brother called one night and told me, based on his last visit, that Mom and Dad need to move. I had been saying the same thing for the past several years but to no avail. I always strove to honor their wishes. The fact is, I could not legally or ethically force them to move. All I could do was suggest, beg, and plead. But Mom especially was dug in. My brother, besides my wife, is my biggest supporter. However, with my fragile emotions, the phone call made me doubt myself again. Was I doing enough? Should I force the issue? What else could I be doing? With Dad's decline, Mom's resistance, and the overwhelming burden I was feeling, I prayed a lot and cried often.

I continually tried talking to Mom but got the expected response; "things are fine, and a move would kill Dad." The situation down there was really killing me. Neither parent was doing well. I trusted the Lord for the right attitude. I felt resentful, believing my mom especially was being selfish and unrealistic, and I didn't want to project on my parents, even though they were partly responsible for this situation. Still, I love them and wanted what is best for them.

I tried not to let the circumstances steal my joy. The Lord reminded me that as I was supporting my parents, I was serving the least of these. I continued to cling to Galatians 6:9 and constantly examine myself to ensure that my motives are pure.

In late November I had an extended visit at Mom and Dad's. Mom had a scheduled colonoscopy, and I visited the day before to ensure that she had everything needed for the preparation. Dad was really going downhill; he struggled to express himself and could not comprehend things being said. He was doing crazy things such as placing his keys in the trash. Dad tried to keep it hidden but he also struggled with incontinence. He was also very depressed, but I was grateful for the few happy moments we had.

Dad was also not eating well but I could always coax him into a meal of roast beef sandwiches and macaroni salad, items I brought from a local shop here in Pennsylvania. I loved that he enjoyed the meals we brought. Diane would also bake homemade cookies for Dad, which he loved. Each time I visited I would also pick up bagels at a shop near I-81 in Virginia. Mom loves bagels and could not get them in her area. I did whatever I could to bring my parents some joy.

Thankfully, their friend Norman agreed to stay with Dad while I took Mom to the hospital for her procedure. I did not want Dad to be left alone. Prayers were answered as she came through the colonoscopy without any issues. She and Dad are both colon cancer survivors so clean results are always a blessing. As she lay there in recovery, still not quite awake, I was taken in by her beauty. In spite of everything, the Lord gently reminded me of how precious my parents are. Many who no longer have their parents would give anything to spend one more day with them. I shouldn't complain. God has given me a gift and I need to be more grateful and look past the circumstances and negative words. The storm has been long and difficult and there have been good moments and days. I need to keep my eyes on the Son.

When Mom and I returned from the hospital, Dad was in a panic. He couldn't find his money which he typically misplaced, claiming that someone stole it. Obsession and paranoia were two behaviors which were increasing. Fortunately, Norman helped Dad find the money roll which stabilized him, for the moment anyway.

I said goodbye to my parents and headed towards home. On my way out of town I stopped at the local diner where my parents had enjoyed dinner so many times. It wasn't the same without them there, but I was blessed to see the manager and Sami, Mom and Dad's favorite server. These wonderful people are my friends, too.

Sam asked how my parents were doing and I gave her the details about their health and circumstances. She listened intently and was very empathetic. She considered my parents not only loyal customers but friends as well. She encouraged me and said, "Bob, you're doing all of the right things for Mom and Dad." With all the chaos and negativity it was hard for me to see beyond the trials. I've found that the right words at the right time are a tremendous blessing. I held back tears at her kind words. They were just what I needed after another stressful trip. And God sent people like Sam to me at the exact times I needed a word of encouragement. I thank Him for this and the many other moments He has blessed me in the midst of the storm.

Chapter 9: A December to Remember (Or Perhaps Forget)

Whoever dwells in the shelter of the Most High will rest in the shadow of the Almighty. I will say of the Lord, "He is my refuge and my fortress, my God, in whom I trust."

Psalm 91:1-2

On December 5th, 2023, I was back in Virginia. Diane accompanied me on the trip. Based on Dad's behavior and Mom's needs around the house, my visits became more frequent. I was in the living room talking with Mom when Dad came up from his office, crying. Since the strokes Dad had become more emotional but this was so not like him. Dad never cried when I was younger so it's still difficult for me to process this behavior. Yet there was something endearing about it.

He sat down in his chair, and I asked, "Dad, what's wrong?" He said, "I love you so much." It was hard to hold back the tears then as it is now as I write this. I've never heard those words from Dad quite like that. And in Dad's final months, when I would say that I love him, his response was typically "okay," but I know that his feelings for me ran much deeper. He was not who he used to be, but his heart was soft at that moment. And it's moments like these that I choose to remember now that Dad is gone.

The next day was totally chaotic. Diane and I stayed overnight at the hotel, about twenty miles away, and arrived back at the house first thing in the morning. Mom was in a panic. "He wants his hair cut but can't drive there; he's throwing things." I offered to take Dad to the barber, but he angrily refused. Mom said, "He doesn't want to go because his hair is dirty." I talked Dad into letting Mom wash his hair which he reluctantly agreed to do. I then took him for a haircut, but he was not happy at first. Then he calmed down, somewhat. After the haircut he handed the barber a $20 bill and then tried to hand her another $20 after she made change. I gently made sure that she had a nice tip but kept Dad from giving away an excessive amount of cash. It was clear that Dad could easily be taken advantage of in his state of mind.

We got back to the house, and I tried to do some financial stuff for them. The routine was, Mom would collect the mail and save bills for me to pay. I did what I needed to do and then went out to feed the animals, intending to head home after I finished with the chores. When I completed the work and was preparing to leave, Mom met me at the door and said that Dad refused to eat and was being nasty towards her. I didn't want to leave under those circumstances so I offered to call the doctor for Mom; if we could get an emergency appointment perhaps Dad's meds could be adjusted to calm him down. At first Mom said that she preferred to wait until Dad's scheduled appointment in January. But things got worse with Dad's behavior, and I was concerned about their safety. Ultimately Mom asked me to make the call. It was clear that Diane and I were not going home anytime soon.

Unfortunately, the doctor wasn't seeing patients that day. But thankfully, she agreed to see Dad if we could get to the office, about twenty-five minutes away, quickly. I praise God, again, for the way He met our needs in amazing, unexpected ways. At first Dad refused to go at Mom's behest so I tried talking to him. He cursed at me and was very combative: "Some family I have, you just want to put me in a home, this is all your mother's fault." "Dad, I just want us to talk with the doctor. I just want her to examine you and maybe change up your meds. I promise I'm not putting you in a home." Little did I know I would eventually be forced to break that promise. One thing I've learned is that this isn't a promise one can always keep depending on how serious the health of your loved one becomes. There could come a point where your loved one requires more care than a family member is capable of providing.

After a lot of weeping and gnashing of teeth, telling Dad I love him and trying to convince him that I only wanted what's best, I drove him and Mom to the doctor. It was a tense trip. All the while he refused to talk to Mom or let her touch him. And he did his share of cursing and complaining under his breath. I prayed silently and wondered how in the world this could ever have a happy ending.

Doctor "H" was wonderful. She was compassionate, empathetic and understanding. She knew Mom and Dad well. They had been seeing her for years, so she was very familiar with their conditions and situation. The doctor sat us in a circle and allowed Dad, Mom, and then me to give our perspectives on what was going on. Dad spoke first, inarticulately but clearly enough to know what was troubling him. He was obsessed with protecting Mom. It turns out that he, rightfully so, was worried about Mom's safety on the farm. He was not comfortable with her being out in the pastures alone, feeding and caring for the large farm animals. As it was, she had previously fallen and injured herself, so Dad's fears were justified. He would sit in his office, feeling helpless, as he watched Mom accomplish the chores. He was terrified that she would get injured. He was ready to change his circumstances. He was ready to move.

Mom, as expected, gave her "I'm fine and just want things to stay as they are" speech. She wants what she wants, living there with Dad not "on her back." Relocating and downsizing were not in her vocabulary.[3] Based on my observations, strictly opinion, Mom was totally out of touch with reality. I understand that people want to stay in their homes as long as they can. I'm not in her shoes and, as stated earlier, I don't know what I'll be like if I make it to my eighties. Therefore, I try not to judge too harshly. However, we were at a critical juncture with Dad's and her health. Something bad was going to happen, it was just a matter of time. The good doctor knew this as well.

Although this storm has affected my thinking, I still consider myself to be somewhat in my right mind. To that end, I have informed my children to "do whatever they need to do" in the event that I am a burden or can no longer care for myself. I may even push back if/when I get to that stage, but I want my children to live their lives. God has blessed me, an unworthy sinner, so much more than I deserve and I have lived a full life.

I know Dad, and, if he had been in his right mind, would not have wanted me to be doing everything I'm doing to support Mom and him. Up until he left this earth Dad would say to me, "You're doing too much…" But it's what he would be doing if the roles were reversed. More than that, I believe it's what God has called me to do.

---

[3] I am grateful that Mom regularly sees a psychiatrist. He uses the word "rightsizing" as opposed to "downsizing." I prefer his word!

When the doctor asked for my perspective, I stated that the status quo was unsustainable. Between the chaos at their home, their health, safety, Dad's behavior, and Mom's living in denial, I was at wits end with the long drive, the continual visits, the unpredictability and the turmoil. I told the doctor that this was a ticking time bomb which was about to explode.

After listening to each perspective, the doctor got really serious with my parents, looked directly at them, and laid out what I'd been telling them for years, and more vehemently over the past few months: First, their safety is paramount. The doctor told them that they were in danger of injuring themselves based on their health and the setup of their home and property. One thing Mom had always told me, even when her mind was sharp, is to never place her in a nursing home or assisted living. I have taken her wishes seriously; none of us wanted to see Mom and Dad in a nursing home. But the doctor told them in no uncertain terms: "If they were to fall and break something, a hip for example, they would end up somewhere they don't want to go." This prediction would eventually come true for both of them...

Second, they immediately should downsize and plan to move to a smaller one-story place with more convenient services, closer to family, for a better life. Dad appeared to take the doctor's advice to heart. For Mom, it went in one ear and out the other. Mom's response was, "I want this, and I need that..." The doctor patiently responded that Mom needed to compromise and make sacrifices given the circumstances. The farm was too big, too isolated and too dangerous for two people in their eighties. Their home had stairs leading to the front door and leading into Dad's office; both became nearly impossible for my parents to safely navigate. Based on the doctor's experience with elderly patients, she asserted that it would be an adjustment for my parents but, in the end, a downsized simpler life would be much better for them. Staying where they were could literally be fatal.

Looking back, Dad recognized that the status quo could not continue and was willing to move all along. Again, I understand that change is difficult, but Mom was in denial. Ironically, she complained constantly about life on the farm, but she didn't want to budge.

I was frustrated and hurt at what transpired after I left. Mom contacted friends and other family members, seeking advice that lined up with her opinions and wishes. I was the bad guy. She also called and complained to the agency about the caregiver and cost, jeopardizing the support and stability I had there. The caregivers were my lifeline (and hers too)! I had to smooth things over with the agency so that there were no hurt feelings. The doctor told Mom that the caregiver support was essential but no matter. I felt like nothing I'd done had been appreciated or heeded, though I had their best interests at heart. I had to remember to not grow weary doing good and to not give up, no matter what arrows were being slung at me. But I'm human and it was difficult.

I prayed this prayer: "Lord, help me lovingly deal with this. In one way I feel like maybe I won't panic now when I get a phone call from Virginia. By being here so much I've made them dependent on me and Mom isn't going to budge. If they, (specifically Mom), think they can handle this themselves, let's see. Talking to and trying to reason with my mother about her reality has been frustrating. For now, I feel like I'll continue to watch their finances and do their taxes, but I won't run down here for every 'crisis.' The best thing, according to their doctor, is to relocate closer to us. Until Mom is ready to accept that and sacrifice something, I can't keep enabling this. Please help me to lovingly help my parents without enabling them to stay in a bad situation."

My assertion that I wouldn't "run down there for every crisis" was an unrealistic thought. The walls were about to come crashing down and I would practically be living there. If I thought that life was upside down before, things would become tantamount to a runaway train which derails.

On the ride home from our visit, Diane and I stopped to do some Christmas shopping. While she was in the store, Dad called her. Dad loved and trusted my wife, so it was heartwarming that he called her for a listening ear. He was frantic! He sobbed and said, "I can't do this! I know I am going to die today! They are going to take everything! I am so scared!" She lovingly tried to calm him down by pointing out that we love him and would not let anything happen to him. He seemed a little better as they finished the conversation.

The next day was Sunday the 11th of December. It began like any other day but would quickly turn into a nightmare. Early in the day, Dad called Diane while we were on our way home from church. Again, he sobbed and reiterated his fear that someone was going to take everything, and he was not going to make it. To this day I don't know what precipitated Dad's paranoia, but something did. Once again, she was able to calm him down for the moment.

Dad called Diane again later that afternoon. This time he was more frantic than the times before. He said he was going to die. He said everything has gone wrong and that he doesn't want to live! She could tell something was different this time. He sounded desperate and almost incoherent. He hung the phone up abruptly, still sobbing. Diane told me that she was worried.

Shortly after that, Mom called and said that Dad was going crazy. He was in his office throwing things. Now Diane and I were both very worried. She texted Mom and said, "Are things okay?" Mom simply responded, "No!" Diane then called Mom's cell phone. Mom somehow answered the call but didn't realize it. We could clearly hear their conversation and became remote witnesses to a horrific situation unfolding in Virginia.

I could hear Mom saying, "Put the gun down, put the gun down!" Evidently Dad was pointing a pistol at his head and waving it around while Mom tried to convince him to drop the weapon. To say that I was terrified and felt helpless would be the understatement of the century. I was five hours away and couldn't get Mom's attention on the phone. Is this how things were going to end?

My instincts told me to call their local sheriff immediately, but I was apprehensive at first. I know Dad's personality and, in his state of mind, if he saw law enforcement coming up his long driveway with lights blazing and sirens roaring, he may go over the edge and that would be it. Dad, in his right mind, would never harm anyone. But God only knows what was going on in his head. His growing irrational behavior, paranoia, and emotions, perhaps coupled with medicine he'd been prescribed, may have triggered this action. I am not a doctor so I can't speculate what was going on. We will never know but one thing was for sure: Dad was out of control and a potential tragedy was unfolding.

I was literally shaking and in the midst of a panic attack. I called my brother who is in law enforcement himself and told him what was going on. I knew that I needed to call the local sheriff in Virginia and every moment counted. My brother confirmed that the protocol was to call the police, but this was our father. We briefly discussed the "what ifs" and quickly agreed that I needed to call the sheriff. Importantly, I needed to be extremely careful in how I described the situation so that no harm would come to my parents or law enforcement.

I called the sheriff's office, gave the details of what was going on as well as Dad's condition, and pleaded with them to handle him with care. Things could potentially go so wrong. They recommended that Mom get out of the office where Dad was. I eventually got a hold of her and asked her to get out of the house, but she insisted on remaining with Dad. I told her that the sheriff was on his way. Then, I waited. I'm sure that only minutes passed but it seemed like hours. Time seemed to stand still as we had no idea what was unfolding in Virginia. I prayed that this would not end in tragedy.

My heart jumped when the phone rang. It was the sheriff. I was relieved when he started the conversation with, "We're here, your Mom and Dad are safe, and everything is under control." The sheriff, who knew Dad well, ensured that the gun had been confiscated and that the medics were called to take him to the hospital which was about thirty miles from their home. I was relieved—for the moment. I was praying and hopeful that Dad would get the help he needed at the hospital. I cannot express my appreciation enough for how the sheriff handled the situation and how he kept in touch with me for weeks later.

That evening, I received a call from the ER. They needed information which neither Dad nor Mom was able to provide. Dad did not know his birth date, nor could he answer basic questions. I was able to fill in the blanks for the hospital. I wondered, "Lord, what are we going to do? This is a nightmare. And just in time for the holidays…"

Obviously, I fully intended to head to Virginia very early the next morning. I assumed that Dad would be admitted to the hospital and hoped that he would be given appropriate medication and perhaps a psychiatric evaluation. I was getting ready for bed when Mom called me in a panic. She said that Dad was being discharged from the hospital. While that was shocking enough, she then demanded that I come down immediately to pick him up. I first questioned why Dad was being discharged so quickly because I feared for Mom's safety if he came home. What would keep him from doing this again? I wanted to talk to a doctor before Dad was released.

Due to the late hour, I told Mom that I would be there first thing in the morning; I planned to come down anyway given the circumstances. Mom was hysterical, insisting that I needed to be there right now. I calmly reminded her that I live five hours away, it was late at night, I didn't have an airplane, and I was tired and in no condition to drive five hours in the dark. Moreover, by the time I would have packed and got on the road, I wouldn't arrive until three or four in the morning. Mom said that she was going to call around and get someone to take her to the hospital to bring Dad home. At one point she irrationally said she was going to call their financial advisor who lives in New Jersey (she only knew his business number and it was a Sunday night). I finally convinced her to calm down and reassured her that the ER would hold him until I arrived in the morning.

On December 12th, I left my house at around 4:30 a.m., apprehensive about what I would be facing that day. At approximately 6:00 a.m., as I was heading south on I-81 in Virginia, my cell phone rang. The caller ID indicated that it was Mom, and I assumed that she was calling to find out where I was so that Dad could be picked up. Was I ever mistaken. Mom said, "I fell out of bed and cut my lip. It's bleeding badly. The ambulance is on its way." She was going to the same hospital where Dad was. I told her I would be there as soon as I could. I also told her to ensure that the house was secure before she left. My plan was to stop by their home and meet up with the caregiver who was scheduled to show up at 9:00 a.m. I didn't know what I would be facing at the ER, so I wanted the caregiver to accompany me to the hospital and assist me in getting Dad and Mom home. I prayed that everything would work out.

A little before 9:00 a.m. I was still enroute to my parents' when the caregiver called. "Where are your Mom and Dad?" I told her what had happened and that I wanted her to come to the hospital with me. I asked, "Are you outside the house?" She replied, "No, I came in when no one answered because I was concerned." Evidently Mom never asked the medics to lock the house, which would have been a simple task. This could have been disastrous if someone had entered the home, robbing the place or harming the caregiver or myself. Just being honest: I was so concerned about my parents but also a bit angry that the house was left unsecured. I thought, "How in the world could my parents keep living on their own there?"

I arrived at the house and picked up the caregiver, Kaye, who I met for the first time in person. I checked around the home to ensure that it was safe, locked the door, set the security alarm, and drove thirty miles to the hospital with Kaye. I anticipated that I would need her help since both parents needed to be discharged and transported home. Unbeknownst to both Mom and Dad, they were in ER rooms right next to each other. You can't make this stuff up!

I saw Mom first. She had six stitches in her lip. Mom told me that she had taken a new prescription to help her sleep, and it caused her to fall out of bed. I asked Kaye to stay with Mom and help with her discharge while I insisted on talking to a doctor about Dad. I wanted to know why he wasn't admitted after the incident the previous night. In my opinion, he would be a danger to himself and Mom. Based on the events of the previous day, he needed serious help.

The doctor was very sympathetic but told me something I would hear continually from health care professionals in Virginia: Based on Dad's condition, the doctor said that they couldn't admit him to the hospital. He either had to go home or into some type of assisted living. The doctor told me that Dad's issue was physical not mental. They speculated that he might have some type of cognitive issue, but the hospital was not equipped to deal with it. If he had a diagnosed psychological issue, there were avenues we could explore. But with his condition, he was coming home.

I was incredulous and very fearful! "What was to keep Dad from doing this again?" I didn't want to bring him home yet and I knew that finding a nursing home or assisted living facility there would take time. Suitable facilities were a distance from my parents' place and there were waiting lists to be admitted. So, we were between a rock and a hard spot.

The medical staff apologized but told me that their hands were tied. I don't know if this is true in other states, but it seems like there are no easy medical solutions in their area when it comes to memory and brain disorders. I was encouraged by several health care professionals that they are working with the government to facilitate better care when it comes to dementia and Alzheimer's disease. However, this wasn't helping me right now.

Kaye loaded Mom into the car, and I took care of Dad. Surprisingly, he was lucid and in good spirits. I drove him and Mom home, slightly annoyed thinking about the times I asked them to downsize and relocate. I gently suggested that this should be a warning sign before something worse happens. Mom got angry with me: "You're not ripping me from my home, we are fine." This should have been a wake-up call, but Mom was still adamant about maintaining the status quo. "I'm fine and don't need help" is her go-to mantra when she is not in the midst of a difficult situation. I was exhausted, frustrated, and apprehensive about the future as we drove back to my parents' house.

After this incident with Dad, my suggesting turned into pleading with them to downsize and relocate, for their own sake but for mine as well. Over the past two years I had grown increasingly concerned that they should move before it was too late. Now here we were...

After we returned from the hospital in the early afternoon, I got Mom and Dad situated in the home and Kaye was there with them. After the long early-morning drive coupled with the stress of the day, I was totally exhausted and literally had nothing left in the tank. My plan was to feed the farm animals, head to the hotel to get a good night's sleep and drive home the following morning.

After I finished feeding the animals and prepared to head to the hotel, some things were said that hurt me deeply. I've learned through this storm that misunderstandings and conflict can and do occur in families when it comes to caregiving. That said, God can, did, and still does use negative and hurtful incidents for His purposes and glory. And I have made mistakes and am not guiltless when it comes to my reactions to situations.

For years I had pleaded with my parents to downsize and relocate I could not legally force them to move nor would I. For now, I was doing the best I could to support my parents, and the caregiver agency was standing in the gap when I couldn't be there. Dad's incident was very fresh, and I was still trying to process it all. My plan was to keep my parents safe and get Dad the help he needed.

The future was so uncertain, and the distance just exacerbated the situation. Whenever family members and friends have offered their help, most times it didn't work out because of their availability and schedules. "I need help on Tuesday" is met with, "Well, I can't make it then, but I can be there Saturday or sometime next week." The crises I've faced and my parents' need for help came on suddenly, when it was not convenient for the helper. "Mom needs someone this afternoon, or tomorrow morning…" That's a tough ask for anyone, especially when parents live in the middle of nowhere and their kids can't just drop what they are doing. They have to put food on their tables and pay their bills, too. Supporting my parents meant that I had to be extremely flexible and also do things by the book.

I confer with my siblings for big decisions regarding Mom and Dad's health. Based on my parents' wishes, I am responsible for making final decisions and commitments. While I have a handle on their health, financial, and administrative needs, the kind of help I need most is companionship for my parents and moral support. I am so grateful for those who have come beside us and provided friendship and companionship for Mom.

After the turmoil from December 12th, I headed home the following day. During my drive home Dad called, crying and insisting that he was being held hostage. I had no way of knowing exactly what was going on because Dad was paranoid, emotional, and confused. When I spoke to Mom, she claimed that "everything was fine." I knew that Dad was not fine and did not have peace about the situation in their home.

I prayed this on 12/15/2022 – "Father, I really would give anything, in my fleshly mind, to not have to deal with all of this. I want and need nothing; just keeping my parents safe, pain-free, and as happy as possible under the circumstances. I don't know how to deal with this, Lord. It's affecting me physically and mentally. Please, Holy Spirit, give me the perspective I need and the strength to do what's right, to not worry, to keep my witness. I don't want this to kill me. Help me to be empathetic but not to get overwhelmed with panic. Please restore my health. I want my life to bring You glory. Thank You for the prayers of Your people."

Chapter 10: The Tempest Knocks Me to the Ground

I would hurry to my place of shelter, far from the tempest and storm.

Psalm 55:8

There is an old Merle Haggard song I felt like I was living out in real time: "If We Make It Through December." I was in the midst of a nightmare with my parents. My level of stress was off the charts. I didn't know if I could take much more.

To this day I don't know what was going through Dad's mind, but he was about to do something which would drastically impact our lives forever. A few days after his "gun incident," he first called me and later called Diane, crying, desperate, and not making any sense. These days this was pretty typical behavior for Dad. We had a caregiver at the house with Mom and Dad, so we assumed that things were under control.

That same night, my cell phone rang, and the caregiver was on the other end: "Rob, I tried to stop him, but your Dad somehow got a knife and cut himself. I had everything hidden but he got a hold of one—somewhere. He's bleeding all over the place." Because Dad is on blood thinners due to Atrial Fibrillation (AFib) and two strokes, the situation described to me was horrible. I was terrified because I remembered his past incident with hedge trimmers and how difficult it was for doctors to stop the bleeding. I was numb and could only say in a choked-up voice, "Call 911!" Thankfully she had already called and said that the sheriff and medics were enroute to my parents' house.

I was on the phone late into the night with the sheriff and the ER. Dad was transported to a hospital forty-five minutes away, supposedly because it had a psychiatric unit. I was encouraged that he finally might get the help he needed. However, I was quickly disappointed when it appeared that, once again, the hospital intended to just send him home without admitting him. I prayed as I often did: "Lord, please help me! Mom cannot handle this!" The sheriff told me that he had seen this scenario before, and Dad would likely be sent home and just do the same thing again. I couldn't believe that this was happening.

I felt guilty that I wasn't there. I was overwhelmed at the magnitude of this storm. Dad's health, Mom's health, the distance, the animals, finances, safety, and what might happen. Not to mention what I was neglecting with my own home and family. I felt that my life was totally out of control. Then I sensed the Lord speaking as the storm raged around me. The truth is: He didn't call me to worry or be anxious. He did not give me a spirit of fear, but of power, love and a sound mind (2 Timothy 1:7). Thank God for His Word!

I'd already made close to twenty, five-hour trips this year and had done my best, though imperfectly, to support my parents. I made up my mind to simply do what I could out of love for them, but could not continue at this pace. It was affecting my health and family. I prayed, "Help me to be compassionate while being rational and reasonable. I am mourning Dad's decline and praying he doesn't come home." The sad truth is, I had lost the Dad I once knew.

Obviously, I had to head back to Virginia immediately. The morning after this latest incident I made the five-hour trip and picked Mom up at her home. We then travelled forty-five minutes to the hospital where Dad was in the ER. He had cuts on his wrist and a large laceration on his chest. He looked like he'd been on the losing end of a bar fight. It didn't seem real.

While Mom and I were with Dad at the hospital, the nurse from the home health agency called to get my account of what happened the night before. She also informed me that the caregiver who wrestled the knife from Dad had to be tested because Dad's blood made its way onto her. That was disturbing enough and just added to my already-high level of stress. But the nurse also gave me some words of encouragement which I desperately needed to hear. She was very understanding and compassionate, and told me that I was doing all of the right things for my parents. Once again, I praised the Lord for sending someone into my life to speak words I needed to hear, just at the right time. As low as I felt on this fast-moving train, the appropriate words gave me a sense of peace in the moment.

Privately, I spoke to Mom and Dad's attorney to see if there was any way I could force Mom and Dad to move, for their sake and mine. The situation was out of control, and they simply weren't safe. I needed to get Dad to a place where he could get help. God forbid if the system failed Dad and he were to be sent home again. I already knew the answer, but the attorney confirmed that my parents controlled the decision to stay or relocate. I understand why the laws are the way they are. Sadly, elder abuse is rampant and there are children, family members, and others who will take advantage of vulnerable elderly people. But what does one do in cases like this? My Mom was dug in and a tragedy was going to happen if Dad came home. And in spite of what she thought, she was in no condition to live alone, especially isolated on a rural farm. Future events would prove this to be true.

Dad was in the ER for almost a week. You read that correctly: In the ER, not a hospital room, for the better part of a week! He was kept in the ER, with little privacy or dignity, awaiting a psychological evaluation. We were in a waiting game with no answers for an outcome. I could not blame the hospital. It was clear that something wasn't right with the "system."

I was upset for Dad and terrified that he would be sent home. Back in 2016, after his major stroke, Dad spent a week in a nursing home/rehab facility in southern Virginia. It was not best experience. No offense to any facilities there but conditions were subpar, in my opinion, given his medical condition. Experts have told me that one must be close to a city to get adequate specialized care. I had tried to get Dad into a stroke facility in a larger Virginia city but his case was not deemed "serious enough." I wondered how much worse a "serious" case would look. We didn't have a lot of options then or now. I prayed that we could get Dad to the right place for the help he desperately needed. I know others have it much worse, but this seemed like the hardest thing I'd ever been through.

On December 20th, Mom and I visited Dad in the ER. He was really sad and confused but knew who we were, which was encouraging. It was heartwarming to observe his affection towards Mom and to hear his desire to see his grandkids. The hospital told me that they were hopeful that Dad would get a bed in a psychiatric hospital, but it could be anywhere in the state of Virginia. Even though I wondered how we would manage logistically and financially, this was an answer to prayer, and I felt temporary relief. I believed that, as long as he could be treated and perhaps live a better life, I would accommodate any situation we faced.

Doctors told me that ultimately it would be best if we could get Dad into a facility close to family, specifically an assisted living/memory care facility. Privately they told me that Dad would get better care in my state (Pennsylvania) given his condition. I asked Dad what he wanted to do. If he wanted to live close to my brother or sister, I would request their consent and help make it happen. Dad was insistent and reiterated that he wanted to live near me and his grandchildren. I wasn't sure how we would accomplish that but I was thankful that Dad was willing to relocate. Moreover, he would be much closer to my brother, sister and their children as well, which would hopefully facilitate more family visits.

Mom expressed her desire to be with Dad, wherever he went, and agreed to move close to me if we could find a suitable place. This dovetailed with their wishes we had discussed in prior years. Could things finally be turning around? Was Mom finally realizing that things needed to change? Not just yet ... She still wanted things to remain as they were. But given the circumstances, and what was to come, life as she knew it, was over. Thinking about it now, life changed for Diane and me as well. "Normal" has been something different ever since ...

I decided to leave for home on the 21ˢᵗ because of an impending snowstorm. Christmas was also coming, and I longed to see my three girls who I had not seen in months. I remembered a journal entry from 2016, when Dad had his second stroke. It read something like: "I'm living in a nightmare." Now, six years later, I felt the same way.

Before leaving for home, I took Mom to see Dad, still isolated in the ER. I was encouraged that Dad was on a video call with a psychiatrist. Mom and I were not permitted to be on the call and had to wait outside of the room. I assumed that Dad would be placed in a hospital that could help him. When the session ended, Mom and I were allowed to enter the room. Dad was crying and sad the entire time. From what I could gather he was humiliated that he could not answer many of the questions asked of him. I'm sure that his isolation in the ER only added to his sadness.

After the call ended, the psychiatrist contacted Mom on her cell phone. After a brief conversation she said, "Please talk to my son," and handed the phone to me. Dad had been in the ER for five days and to my astonishment the psychiatrist repeated the same thing I had heard before: "Your father's problem is physical, not behavioral. There is nothing we can do for him. We are sending him home." I couldn't believe my ears! Not again! He'd been in the ER for a week and this is what we get? It's only through the Holy Spirit's help that I kept my cool and did not let anger rule my speech. Again, I can't blame the hospital or doctors and don't pretend to understand all how all of this was supposed to work.

I pleaded with the doctor, informing him that Mom could not care for Dad because of his erratic, unpredictable behavior; he was at risk to likely harm himself again and potentially Mom as well. The doctor said that our best bet was to place him in a memory care or assisted living facility, but I knew that it would take time. What do we do with Dad in the meantime? In addition to his and Mom's safety, if he came home, it would be difficult to convince him to leave for a memory care facility. I felt helpless and ready to give up. I believe that the next words out of my mouth were from God, Himself: I said to the doctor, "Are you aware that Dad had two strokes? Does that play any role in this?"

For reasons I do not know nor can explain except by God's intervention, my comments did make a difference. The doctor agreed to do some research and said he would call me back. Before I headed home, the doctor called, as promised. He stated that there was one hospital in the state of Virginia which would admit Dad: a facility about thirty miles from his home. From the sound of it, I sensed that this would not be the perfect place. But it would at least keep him from coming home and buy us some time until we could get him into a specialized facility near me in Pennsylvania.

At this point I was practically living in southern Virginia. Since the ultimate plan was to get Dad into memory care close to us, my wife was doing research in Pennsylvania. Diane contacted a number of facilities near our home and each one had waiting lists to get in. She toured a memory care/assisted living facility right before Christmas and spoke with the staff. She was impressed with their compassion, empathy, and professionalism, as well as what the facility offered. Moreover, the cost was "reasonable" given comparable facilities. It seemed like the perfect place for Dad. But there were two impediments facing us: First, there was a waiting list so it was unknown when he could be admitted. Second, with Dad's history and the attempts to harm himself, we were unsure if the facility would accept him. That would have to be determined later, in coordination with the hospital in Virginia.

Meanwhile, because of Dad's history and hospital rules, law enforcement would supervise his entry and hopefully eventual dismissal from the hospital. I felt terrible that this was our only option at the time because I did not believe that Dad would purposely harm himself or anyone. He obviously had a disease. His recent behavior was not like him, and I felt that the right medical care could stabilize him. I prayed and had hope that memory care and the right medicines would at least allow him to live a better life.

The sheriff called and gave me the option to transport Dad to the hospital. I declined because I needed to get home with the impending weather and the Christmas holiday. Also, it would have broken my heart to say goodbye to Dad and release him into an unknown situation. Sadly, no one would be allowed to visit Dad in the hospital for a period of seven days, nor could we have any contact with him during that time. All of this was right around the holidays…

So, the sheriff agreed to pick Dad up and drive him to the hospital. I was thankful that Dad was not placed in shackles which had been a distinct possibility. The sheriff told me that he had a nice talk with Dad on the long ride. Dad always had the ultimate respect for law enforcement and had many friends in the profession over the years. During the ride, there were several moments where Dad was confused. Dad told the sheriff that he (Dad) was 108 years old. So sad. I prayed that he would be safe and that we were doing the right thing, but I didn't have peace about it. Still, what choice did we have? My emotions were all over the place.

After the sheriff transferred Dad to the hospital, he called and told me this was not the best place for Dad, in his opinion. I held back tears when the sheriff said, "Bob, if this were my dad, I would not let him stay there long."

Hindsight really can be 20/20. I think it was Mike Tyson who said, "Everyone has a plan until they get punched in the mouth." The storm was raging, I lived five hours away, and we literally had no options short of Dad coming home. He could not be home for even one night, so we needed an immediate solution, like it or not. And nothing in this realm is ever easy or expedient.

As it turned out, Dad would remain in that hospital for a total of forty days which still haunts me. I wish there could have been a different solution but there wasn't. I still find it hard to fathom that he spent so long there. He would continually and sadly tell me that "he was never getting out of the hospital," and at times I wondered myself if he might be correct. But on the positive side, he did receive good medical care and Physical/Occupational therapy and eventually would be released. But it was a bumpy road…

Before Dad was transported to the hospital, I took Mom to a local restaurant in Virginia for dinner. As we were finishing up, I overheard two ladies talking about geriatric care and dementia. Once again, I sensed God doing something in the midst of the storm. What are the chances that these women, who obviously had expertise in this area, were sitting in this rural restaurant at this moment, having this discussion? I never cease to be amazed at how God provides just the person we need at the right time! I found out that one of the women is a social worker who deals with elder care and dementia as a career. I got her attention, and she graciously agreed to sit and talk with us for a few minutes.

She offered some advice on how to navigate the health care system in Virginia for those suffering with Alzheimer's and dementia. She confirmed that the best plan was to move Dad to a facility near me in Pennsylvania and that was our hope. I was amazed that there seemed to be no clear avenue for people with dementia, though Dad had not been formally diagnosed. She also provided some good counsel on how to advocate for Dad if I ran into roadblocks. She and others I spoke with said that the hospital where Dad was staying was not a bad place. That gave me some comfort, but I still never felt good about it, especially once I had the opportunity to visit Dad there.

I talked to Mom about the current reality and the future. With Dad in the hospital and hopefully destined for a memory care facility in Pennsylvania, Mom finally agreed that she needed to move and wanted to be with Dad. She asked me to look for real estate and specified certain things she wanted in a new house. At that point there was no rush; Mom was relatively healthy, and it was winter, not the best time to shop for a home. The plan was to take our time and perhaps wait to buy a place in the spring. But our plans would be accelerated in the not-too-distant future.

Initially Mom wanted a large piece of land outside of my town to build a new house. That was not the best idea because we would need to be close to Dad as well as medical services. Also, she did not need to be moving to another rural, farm-like situation where she would be tied down with responsibilities and once again isolated from people. In a sense we would be recreating the situation that got us here in the first place. Moreover, buying land and building a house would take months if not longer. A Christian real estate agent/friend confirmed to Mom that she needed a simple, small, one-story place near people and services. Her doctors agreed with that sentiment.

We offered to have Mom stay with us until she found a suitable place, but she insisted on keeping her hound dog. This was a non-starter; we do not have a fence in our yard and she (and we) each have two cats. We looked into an apartment for Mom, but few were available, and none allowed a large active dog. Additionally, our house is two-story and, with what was to come with Mom's health, that would not work for her.

Due to the gravity of this decision and Mom's increasing memory issues, I wrote up an agreement basically outlining her wishes: Her desire to move to Pennsylvania to be near Dad, things she wanted in a new house, and the need to sell her Virginia house and property. I had Mom read and sign it, hoping that I would never need to refer back to it. I also kept her text messages to me from December and January just in case. Sadly, the time would come when Mom would forget the circumstances which necessitated the move.

Sometimes, when she tells the story, Mom often indicates that she never had closure with regard to leaving Virginia. The truth is, Mom agreed to this plan and after the holidays would soon beg me to move her. By the time we executed the move, she was immobile. She also tells people that she went from an eight-day hospital stay in Virginia to a strange new home in Pennsylvania. Mom never had a hospital stay in Virginia and we moved her straight from her Virginia home to the new one in Pennsylvania.

You'll soon read about exactly how the move took place. The thing you'll also learn is that a great deal of what Mom recollects is due to her memory issues. Please understand, as I've stated before, I love my mother dearly and am not disparaging her in any way. The things she has gone through and would go through have seriously affected her physical, mental, and behavioral states. But we were desperate as all of this unfolded and she has forgotten the events which got us here. In addition to her worsening memory issues, it is heartbreaking to see how much physical pain she has endured.

Before I left from Virginia for home I prayed: "Lord, let this work out so that we can get Mom and Dad living near us. Please give Mom strength and clarity as I leave today, protect her Lord. And please protect Dad and impress upon him that he is deeply loved by You and us. This is so hard, and it's Christmas time..."

I finally returned to Pennsylvania on the 22nd of December. I was so grateful to be home just before Christmas, but the holidays would end up being a blur to me.

From the time Dad was admitted to the hospital until the day he was released, I never knew quite what was going on there. At first, we were told that Dad would be kept for thirty days to stabilize him; this seemed like an answer to prayer as we needed time for a bed to open up in memory care near us. However, Mom called me the first night Dad was in the hospital. She said that she received a call from a nurse who told her that Dad purposely banged his head against the wall and was trying to escape. Supposedly the nurse also told Mom that she "better be finding him a place ASAP." I was terrified that Dad would be released prematurely and we'd be right back where we started. When I asked Mom for the name of the nurse who called, she "couldn't remember," causing me to question the validity of the conversation she had with the hospital.

Different people at the hospital would tell Mom conflicting stories at times, but I am basing that statement on what she would convey to me. I continually worried that Dad would be released before we could get him into memory care. As much as I hated Dad being in that hospital, I feared that he would be released to come home which would have been disastrous. We needed time. The leadership of the hospital did step up and give me confidence that Dad would not be released until we had a place near us to transition him to. But it was difficult to know who was responsible for the ultimate decisions regarding his release.

I prayed this prayer. "Father, there is so much going on and so much to do. I have these requests:

1. Please keep Dad alive and healthy.

2. Get him to memory care here which seems like the ideal place.

3. Help us find a house for Mom here

4. Help me with the physical move, bills, address changes

5. Help us to sell Mom and Dad's property

6. Taxes and paperwork

7. Keeping everything straight

8. Mom's mind/health

9. Dad understanding that we love him.

Lord, it's one of the biggest challenges I've ever faced but You have always been faithful. This is my mom and dad. Praying for strength and wisdom."

Looking back, it was very difficult. But God answered that prayer in His timing and in His perfect will.

Chapter 11: Was There a Christmas This Year?

Today in the town of David a Savior has been born to you; He is the Messiah, the Lord.

Luke 2:11

Normally this time of year is one of joy and anticipation. During my career I always looked forward to the Christmas season. I loved celebrating the birth of my dear Lord and Savior, Jesus Christ. I also loved being with family and the "down time" where I could focus on things besides work. But Christmas in 2022 snuck up on me and would be like no other...

This year, 2022, the 23rd of December was dreary and depressing. I sat at the desk in my home where I usually spend a quiet time each morning. Rain and sleet blanketed the area.

The weather reflected how I felt. I kept thinking, "This is one of the hardest times of my life. Yet the joy of the Lord was and is my strength."

Based on a call Mom received the night before, it did not sound like Dad would live much longer. The hospital asked for his Advanced Directive which contains end-of-life wishes should Dad's health get to that point. Mom asked me for guidance. She was depending on me to make critical decisions which was intimidating but humbling. I discussed things with her, filled out the information, and subsequently sent the paperwork to the hospital.

I was sad that Dad was alone, but it didn't sound like he was suffering. He went downhill so quickly and the attempts to harm himself were the tipping point. I was overwhelmed thinking of all that would need to be done but my goal was to keep Mom safe and meet her physical, mental, financial, and all other needs.

I don't know what possessed me to do it, but I actually sat down and wrote Dad's obituary. I didn't think that Mom would be able to do it, and I had learned so much about Dad's life over the past several years. In a way it was healing for me. I longed to remember the Dad I once knew. He lived quite a meaningful life, in spite of many hardships. Interestingly, most of what I wrote remained intact for Dad's actual obituary when he passed nine months later. I slept well for a change, at peace about Dad, and grateful that Mom's caregiver agreed to spend the night with her so she would not be alone. Another example of God providing just what I needed in His perfect timing. Administratively, since Dad was no longer living at home, the caregivers were now assigned exclusively to Mom.

On December 24th I wrote this in my journal:

Christmas Eve 2022. Father, I am desperate for You. No one except You understands what I am going through. People mean well but many of their words are often just unsolicited advice. Help me to live Philippians 4:4-8.

Praying:
- Dad is at peace and in no pain
- If it be Your will, transition him to memory care near us but not home. Please work things out in Your perfect timing.
- Mom be kept safe.
- That we find a suitable home for her here.
- That I can secure/organize her assets to get her moved here.
- That I can handle all of the administrative and financial things.
- That my family will cooperate and support.
- That You provide special wisdom and strength and that my health doesn't suffer.

Please let my mind focus on You, not my circumstances. May I not feel guilty or empathetic to the point that I think I'm responsible for everything. I am not God; I am not Superman.

Isaiah 55:8-9—I don't always understand but I'm trusting You. Draw me close in the midst of this storm.

Christmas this year was "different," that's for sure. It's one I will never forget. I kept reminding myself that the Lord is good and I prayed 2 Chronicles 20:12: "I don't know what to do but my eyes on are You."

I was thankful to have all three of my girls home, but December 25th was not my best day. I'm just being honest. I was totally distracted by the situation in Virginia. Dad was alone in a hospital, and we were not allowed to contact him. Mom was lonely and sad, isolated in her southern Virginia home. She called several times crying because she was alone. We had no caregiver for that day because no one was available on the holiday.

We set up a video call with the family and the focus was all on Mom and her circumstances. Between that and Dad being alone in a hospital, it didn't feel at all like Christmas. I felt badly for my family and prayed that they at least enjoyed the holiday. I also felt terrible about Dad, alone in a strange place, on Christmas Day. I thought, "Lord, I can't go on like this. Please help me, please provide a breakthrough."

The day after Christmas, I was headed back to Virginia. I lost count of the number of trips I had made in 2022. I prayed that something good would happen. I prayed that somehow God would make me a witness and a blessing as I travelled. My plan was to help Mom out, provide her with some companionship, and hopefully visit Dad in the hospital. I prayed constantly that we could get him transitioned to a memory care facility and that he wouldn't be sent home prematurely. I was also praying for my health. I began to hear from trusted friends about the importance of "self-care." I would hear even more about it as things progressed. Unfortunately, while I heard about it, I wasn't practicing it. There was just no spare time to do anything for myself and consequently my health suffered.

Friends would ask me: "How was your Christmas?" While I avoided having my feelings spill out, I would typically respond, "It was fine." In my mind I thought, "Was there a Christmas this year? I must have missed it ..."

Chapter 12: No Good Deed Goes Unpunished

Though the Lord is exalted, He looks kindly on the lowly; though lofty, He sees them from afar. Though I walk in the midst of trouble, You preserve my life. You stretch out Your hand against the anger of my foes; with Your right hand You save me.

Psalm 138:6-7

On December 27th, 2022, I was back in Virginia and took Mom to visit Dad for the first time at the hospital. Before we could show up at the facility, we had to call and make an appointment. This was standard protocol. There were very limited time windows for visits and we were only permitted to be there for an hour. The hospital is locked down and has very strict rules. We had to sign in, leave our photo IDs at the front desk, and be escorted to a room where we could sit with Dad. It was difficult to see him in this condition and it always broke my heart.

We never saw Dad's room so could not ascertain how good or bad his living conditions were. He gave us hints that things were not good, but we were never allowed to venture outside of the prescribed meeting area. We do know that he had at least one roommate and was not allowed any personal belongings in his room. The visits would occur in an old cafeteria, with a staff member supervising us. Dad was glad to see us but very emotional and confused. He kept repeating, "All I want to do is move up to your area and be with my family and grandkids." I promised Dad that we were pursuing that. I didn't tell him that his destination would be memory care in an assisted living facility, but I knew that conditions would be better there than in this hospital. For starters, he would have more independence and socialization. Moreover, he would be close by and I could visit him often.

I wanted to give Dad hope, but it got to a point where he became negative and believed he would never be released. All during his stay he would say, "It's never going to happen, I'll be here for the rest of my life." To be honest, I wasn't sure when and even if he would be released since information was difficult to obtain. But I promised him that we would move him up to Pennsylvania as soon as we could. Based on Dad's situation there was still a process to follow, even after a bed opened up in the memory care facility. A judge would need to formally release him based on recommendations from the hospital.

On the day Mom and I visited Dad, I started to develop a little cough. I didn't think much about it but, the following morning, the cough became stronger. I also developed a fever, headache, extreme fatigue, and pain in my chest. As I drove Mom to the hospital to visit Dad for the second time, the symptoms became progressively worse. I knew that I was coming down with "something." After the thirty-minute drive I pulled in to the hospital parking lot before our appointed time to visit.

I shut the vehicle off and said to Mom, "I really don't feel well and don't want to pass anything on to Dad. You need to go in by yourself. Please tell Dad I'm sorry, I promise I will visit again when I feel better." I didn't say it aloud, but I also feared giving whatever this illness was to Mom.

Mom went into the hospital alone and I remained in Dad's truck. A few minutes later my phone rang. It was Mom and she handed the phone to Dad. "Why don't you want to see me?" he said tearfully. I felt terrible. "Dad, of course I want to see you. I feel very sick and don't want to give this to you or anyone in the hospital, in case I'm contagious. As soon as I feel better, I'll be back. I promise!" I don't think he understood but I reminded him that I loved him very much. I prayed that he would understand.

After Mom came back to the parking lot we headed to her house. I was going downhill quickly and could barely drive. By the time we arrived at Mom's place I was totally fatigued and very ill. I snuck into a back bedroom and tried to fall asleep at about two in the afternoon. At one point Mom came looking for me and was calling my name. I was so tired and sick; I asked her politely to leave me alone and let me sleep. I had absolutely no energy. I didn't wake up until 3:00 a.m. the next morning.

My brother had made his way down from New Jersey and was staying at a hotel in Richmond. The plan was for him to relieve me at Mom's house and take her to visit Dad that morning. This would give me a break for a couple days anyway. I hoped to see my brother for a few minutes that morning, to talk and hand responsibilities over to him. Importantly, I did not want Mom to be alone, even for a minute. No caregiver was scheduled for that day.

A little after 3:00 a.m., I texted my brother and informed him that I was leaving for home. I felt awful and did not want him to catch whatever I had. I've had bad cases of the flu as well as pneumonia in the past. Whatever I had now brought back memories of those experiences. I have no idea where I picked up the "bug," but I had been around hospitals since mid-December so was not surprised.

My memory is a little fuzzy, but I left Mom's house between four and five in the morning. It was very dark and one always has to worry about deer on the roads because the area is very wooded and rural. Looking back, I was in no condition to be driving. I was light-headed and extremely fatigued. However, if I hadn't left when I did, I may have been stuck there; I would not only have infected everyone but also been far from medical care. I just wanted to get home and be in my own bed!

To say that driving in this condition was not my best decision is another huge understatement. Only by the grace of God did I make it about forty-five minutes, when dawn was breaking, and I could go no further. I was extremely weak and tired. I pulled into a grocery store parking lot and tried to sleep for a few minutes. Nothing I did could relieve my symptoms. I had no appetite and could not sleep nor get comfortable. So, I just sat there and tried to rest.

After some time had passed, I drove again and made it as far as a rest stop on Interstate 64. I passed right by my favorite coffee shop along the way, so you know that I wasn't well! My routine always involved a visit to Baines Coffee both to and from my parents' place. But I didn't want to infect anyone and the thought of eating or drinking anything was the furthest thing from my mind.

I tried to sleep some more at the rest stop and remained there for at least an hour. I made one more rest stop around Winchester, Virginia, and finally arrived home at 12:30 p.m. The normally five-hour trip turned into an eight-and-a-half-hour trip. I thanked God for safety because I was not in the best condition to be driving.

Given the symptoms I had a strong suspicion that this could be Covid, especially when I began to lose my sense of taste. We had a few test kits lying around so I opened one, swabbed my nose and waited. Covid was at its peak in 2020 and, while I took necessary precautions, I was not overly cautious about avoiding social situations. Therefore, I was surprised that I never came down with the virus back then. But this test did not lie—I was very positive now.

To add insult to injury, right after I got home my brother called from Virginia and said that both he and Mom were sick. He still visited Dad, but Mom was too sick to make the trip to the hospital. Evidently Dad was in a bad mood and told my brother that "he wants out of the hospital," which made me feel guilty that he was stuck there. As it turned out, Mom got Covid as well but somehow, and miraculously, my brother didn't. He did, however, stumble on a front step as he was leaving my parents' house, and cracked a rib. Yes, you really can't make this stuff up! I wasn't sure how much more I could take. I continued to pray earnestly that things would work out to get both of my parents to Pennsylvania.

Was there a New Year's holiday this year? I must have missed that one, too.

This was my journal entry on New Year's Eve, 2022:

Lord, I am so sick. Throat pain goes all the way up to my ears. So tired, I've lost several pounds. I am lost Lord, hopeless without You. Please do a miracle.

I don't know the mind of God but, looking back, I believe that Covid was a gift in disguise. This seems like a bizarre statement, but I was exhausted and on the verge of burning out. Covid kept me out of Virginia for a couple weeks and forced me to slow down. I could not travel and, though I didn't realize it until now, it gave me a needed break. I thank God that Mom had caregiver support from the agency for most days. And Dad's friend Norman stepped up once again to help Mom around the farm and drive her to visit Dad at the hospital. But this break would be short-lived, and things were about to go up another notch.

Chapter 13: Can Things Get Any Worse?

Truly my soul finds rest in God; my salvation comes from Him. Truly He is my rock and my salvation; He is my fortress, I will never be shaken.

Psalm 62:1-2

New Years Day 2023 was unlike any other. Like the Christmas of 2022 that never was, I will never forget January 1, 2023. With Covid it seemed all I could do was sleep but I was awakened by the fireworks and noise makers at midnight when the new year was ushered in. So many "if onlys" went through my mind: If only Dad hadn't tried to harm himself, if only Mom had agreed to move sooner, if only they didn't live five hours away. This storm was a nightmare and was taking its toll on all of us.

I contacted the caregiver agency to inform them that Mom had Covid. I was surprised but thankful that they still provided support, although they charged a "Covid rate" which was expensive. That was fine with me. I had no options, and Mom could not be left alone.

I kept praying for a breakthrough; that memory care would open up, that we could find a house for Mom, that we could rehome the farm animals, and something new: that Diane would not get Covid. As hard as we tried to isolate ourselves at home, my wife finally got the virus as well.

I prayed that Dad would hang on and make it out of the hospital, and not hold anything against me. I hated that he was there, but we had no other options. I was so weak physically, spiritually, and mentally. I prayed for the Lord to restore me and to somehow be glorified.

I wrote this in my journal on January 2, 2023:

I choose to trust You today, Lord. You have always been faithful and have worked things for my good, even when I don't understand. My circumstances right now are difficult:

1. Diane is in the heart of Covid
2. I am feeling better but not 100%
3. Mom is sick, lonely, and scared. I haven't heard from her since yesterday.

4.	Dad is alone in a hospital. Not sure of his condition.
5.	On a waiting list for memory care. Praying a room opens soon and that transition is smooth.
6.	There are no houses available up here for Mom. Praying something opens up soon.
7.	The distance, the animals, the complexity of their property and stuff.

Lord, I don't see a way out or a happy ending, but You are the God of miracles, the God of the possible.

It was only the 3rd of January, and I was living a surreal life. I prayed that things would ease up in 2023 but it wasn't happening—yet. Dad was still in a Virginia hospital and I had no contact for a number of days due to Covid. I prayed continually that we could get him into memory care here quickly. I also prayed that we could get a house for Mom soon. But there wasn't a lot for sale that met the criteria we needed. One impediment was the fact that she wanted to keep the dog, which limited our choices. Further, two-story houses and anything with steps were out of the question due to her mobility issues. These factors, the time of year, and the ultra-competitive housing market severely limited our choices. I prayed that God would keep Mom safe and in good health. I prayed that He would use me in some way even though I was very fragile.

Despite the circumstances, in my quiet time the Lord reminded me that I had much to be grateful for.

This is what I wrote in my journal:

- Though these past few months, especially the last month, may be the hardest in my life, I choose to be grateful.
- Though I can't see a way out or a happy ending, I choose to be grateful.
- Though I second guess myself and wonder if I've done enough, I choose to be grateful.

You love me, You came for me, You died for me, You rose again for me, You have a bigger plan than I can see. I pray for the strength and wisdom to carry out Your plan and bring You glory.

It took a while for the cough and fatigue to subside. Every day I prayed for at least one breakthrough. Sometimes one came but then five setbacks accompanied it. I hung onto my faith, trusting the Lord the best I could. I prayed for a new vision, new hope. I'd been in the wilderness for a while now. But so have others to a much greater extent. I've learned that some of the best times of worship have been when I am still, in the wilderness. You have always been there for me Lord. You are enough...

Someone once said that God's timing is perfect but seldom early. I've found some truth in that statement. Earlier I mentioned a close friend from our Sunday school class who is a real estate agent. She and her husband are humble, honest people and had empathy for our situation. We trust them and asked for advice in finding a place for Mom. Just as I was getting over Covid our friend showed me a few houses. Mom was finally willing to relocate, so she said, mainly because she wanted to be with Dad. I was discouraged that the homes I saw that day would not suit her. The market was so competitive and supply so limited, that even less-than-suitable homes were listed and sold almost immediately. Oh, and the selling price was almost always more than what was listed. I was hoping to not get into a bidding war.

In the back of my mind, I knew that Mom wouldn't be "happy" with anything here, but I prayed that she would eventually adjust. Although her situation was unsustainable in Virginia, deep down she did not want things to change. To this day she views the "farm" and Virginia as paradise and has difficulty seeing past that. She recalls none of the inconveniences and hardships there, nor how dire her health became.

I prayed that Mom (and Dad) would survive a move up here and that we could pull it off. So many things would need to fall into place to buy a house close to us and sell their massive property in Virginia. The whole process would likely take many months, per our friend, and also the real estate agent we would utilize in Virginia.

Mom talked to Dad and told me that he was much worse. I knew that he wanted to come "home," and he recognized that living in Virginia was no longer viable. I prayed that memory care could become his home and that he would be here soon. I prayed that I could hold myself together and handle everything I needed to do. In addition to their health concerns, I was overwhelmed thinking about the responsibility of managing their finances, selling their property, buying a new house, and moving their household goods. I also became concerned about preparation of their 2022 tax returns which would totally fall into my lap.

I wrote this on January 7th:

Twenty-five years today since Pop (my late grandfather) died. I've been in a major funk since October. Every circumstance, every piece of bad news, every discouragement sends me into a tailspin. This is not Biblical. You have always been faithful. I either trust You or I don't. No matter what, I refuse to conform to the world's ways but rather choose to be transformed by the renewing of my mind. You answered my prayers in a big way yesterday, giving Mom a good visit with Dad. I prayed for peace and You provided just that. Thank You! Peace in this world starts with peace from God. Peace comes from being reconciled to Jesus Christ. I also looked at a house which seems perfect for Mom. I am praying it works out.

On January 9th, I was ready to head to Virginia for another trip but there was snow on the ground and slippery roads. Normally I would leave at four or five in the morning so that I had most of the day to get things done at Mom and Dad's. This day I would leave a little later. On the way I learned that Dad was transported to another hospital overnight for some issue which I never did figure out. Mom told me a bizarre story where Dad was wrapped in tight clothes which resembled a strait jacket. As the story went, the ambulance drove him around and, after a few hours, returned him to the state hospital. With everything that had transpired, nothing surprised me. I didn't know what I'd be facing in Virginia that day. But that had become the norm.

Mom had a nice talk with Dad and the team at the hospital. Between the social worker and head of nursing it seemed like they had Dad's best interests at heart. I also received a call from the memory care facility in my town. They had received the paperwork I submitted at their request and planned to do an assessment of Dad via video call with the hospital. We were still on a waiting list but perhaps things were finally falling into place?

I prayed, "Father, You know my heart. I am only doing what my parents asked me to do. Their wishes, not mine or anyone else's. If I had my wishes, they would have moved a long time ago and we wouldn't be in this situation."

When I arrived in Virginia, I picked Mom up and headed to the hospital. We visited with Dad, and I spoke with the Occupational Therapist who had been working with him. The therapist had Dad walking better but told me that his eyesight needed to be checked once we got him moved to memory care. Evidently, he had trouble reading and his vision was affecting his balance.

Unfortunately, Dad was not having the best day; he was confused and forgetful. As I stated earlier, to this day I have no idea what his life was like in this hospital when we were not there. I just know that Dad was depressed and came to believe that he would never leave the facility. As long as I've known him, Dad was always meticulous about his grooming. He was always clean-shaven with perfectly combed hair. However, the hospital was not shaving him, and he was sporting quite the mustache and beard. His hair was also unkempt. I had never seen him like this, and it made me sad. At some point the facility did finally shave him after I casually commented about Dad's appearance.

I arrived back home on January 14, 2023. That morning, I was up early for my quiet time and actually felt semi-normal, a rare thing these days. So often my mind was racing and distracted, but this morning I had a rich time in prayer and devotions with my Lord. I prayed that He would keep my eyes fixed on Him. He reminded me that I can do all things through Christ Who gives me strength.

On the 15th we had a contract on the purchase of a new house for Mom, a little over three miles from my residence. It was truly miraculous that we were able to get this home so quickly given the market and short supply of houses. Our real-estate agent friend had found what we believed to be the perfect home for Mom. It had just come onto the market and we had the first opportunity to purchase it. I won't get into the details, but the sale was a blessing to both the seller and us.

Mom approved of the house based on pictures and specifications I sent her. She texted this on January 5th: "I like the development. Reminds me of the development we lived in back in New Jersey. I know I am a pain but a development would be better for me." I'm glad that I kept that text. Mom has an idyllic recollection of her place in Virginia and nothing compares to that. Consequently, she does not have much good to say these days about the new house or the development. With her memory and physical issues, coupled with all that she has lost, it's understandable.

The house is part of a quad unit, with one floor, two bedrooms and two bathrooms. A number of seniors live in the neighborhood and love it. People in the development are friendly and go out of their way to be hospitable. I know and converse with a number of them when I'm out for a run or working in Mom's yard. The home was much smaller than what Mom was accustomed to but perfect for a senior with mobility issues. In all honesty, I wish the home itself were a little larger, but choices were few and we were desperate. Additionally, anything bigger would not serve Mom well due to her mobility issues. The truth is, there are things about my home which I wish were a little different. Nothing is perfect.

Her home has many useful features, a number of which were ideal for what was to come. The bathrooms and garage entry have grab bars. The carpeting is thin and easy to navigate. Yet I knew that Mom would not like it whenever she moved here. Prior to moving in, Mom insisted that we install a fence for her dog. We did that, reluctantly. Later she would smartly realize that caring for the dog, in her condition, was not a wise decision. I am grateful that my sister eventually adopted the dog from Mom, but we spent money on a fence we didn't really need.

Just to jump ahead a little, over the past year we added a beautiful sunroom and a walk-in tub (exactly like Mom had in Virginia), and she does enjoy both of those things. I bought a small plaque, dedicating the sunroom to Dad. He was present when we made the purchase and wanted Mom to have it, but sadly he didn't live to see the finished space.

I spoke to Dad on the phone, which was always interesting; I had to call the hospital and wait for a staff member to bring Dad to the community phone. Many times, there was a busy signal because another resident was using the phone. That day Dad was still confused but he didn't sound bad. Mom, however, was another story. This was difficult enough with Dad's condition. Changes were coming. If it were just Dad…

My focus was so much on Dad and keeping Mom afloat in Virginia, that I hadn't noticed the subtle changes in her memory and demeanor. In her defense, her husband was in a hospital, thirty miles away, and she was living alone in a very rural area. She was also preparing to sell her property of more than thirty-three years and move to a strange area. All of these changes would be traumatic for anyone. But as time would go on, those factors could only explain so much.

One night Mom called me at 9:30 p.m., completely off the rails. She was angry and frantic that she could not find the dog's bed. She asked me where it was. I had no idea and could do nothing about it being five hours away. Evidently the caregiver had put it away earlier in the day to reduce clutter, but I had no way of knowing that. I suggested that Mom simply let the dog sleep on the floor. I didn't think that a night without his hair-covered bed would keep the hound from sleeping. But that did little to calm her and she became angry with me. Although Mom's cognitive issues became more evident, I didn't immediately realize what was happening. Dad's condition and issues consumed most of my time and thoughts.

On January 18th, the hospital called Mom. Dad was evidently crying and asking for her. It appeared that he was going downhill rapidly. The caregiver called me and said that Mom was confused and her mind was slipping. I was getting as close to a breakdown as I ever have been—again. Yet, I would have even bigger mountains to climb before too long. I wasn't sure how this was going to turn out and continued to pray that we could get Dad out of that hospital and moved to memory care here, sooner rather than later. I was also very concerned about Mom. Her health, the logistics and financial implications of moving her were all on my mind. Another big concern was how she would react when she relocated. That would be worse than I ever imagined.

I prayed: "Lord, I sit here in Your presence, consumed by the circumstances in Virginia, and I don't know what to do. I need Your physical healing and wisdom to pass this test."

The memory care facility here in Pennsylvania called with a possible transition date for Dad. I went into the office and signed the agreement to admit him. I had prayed and journalled that something would happen this week. I thanked God, that things finally appeared to be coming together.

On January 20th, I woke up in the middle of the night, thinking about the peace of God. I reflected on the previous day when Mom had called, insisting that Dad could move the following Thursday. I wasn't sure how she got that date; the memory care facility had to coordinate with the hospital in

Virginia to agree on when Dad would be released. Tentatively the plan was to transition the following Thursday or Friday but that was not written in stone. Mom's expectations for Dad's release and finding a new house were unrealistic, even though the Lord caused things to happen miraculously quickly. Throughout this storm I have learned that most things take time and nothing is easy.

During the times when I was exhausted and ready to give up, I again recalled the promise to Dad: that I'd get him to Pennsylvania and keep Mom safe. More importantly, God reminded me that I was doing what He called me to do, and I couldn't walk away. All Dad wanted was to be with Mom and his family. I took solace in my faith and the fact that Dad, in his prime, did the same things for his mother and for Mom's parents. Since this storm started, experts and friends have told me that this role would be thankless, and I would be criticized. While I knew that in my head, I'm still human, and it was, and still is, difficult at times.

I spoke with Dad on January 21st. He was actually in better spirits than Mom, though he still believed that he'd never leave the hospital. I tried to convince him that we were close and reminded him of my promise: to get him out as soon as possible. I was praying for the 31st if not sooner. I was also praying that we could keep Mom stable emotionally until we moved her to Pennsylvania.

On the 23rd, Diane and I drove to Virginia. I had things to do at home so, after a short visit, I left Diane with Mom to start preparing for the move. My wife is very organized and could not only help around the house but also provide companionship for Mom. Diane is a saint and very patient, but I prayed that she would be able to deal with Mom and her emotions. On the first day she was there, Diane took Mom to the hospital and had a nice visit with Dad. Dad was also so happy to see my wife for the first time in a while.

Meanwhile, back home, I completed the paperwork in order to admit Dad into memory care. Before Dad had his incidents back in December, he misplaced and discarded several important records. I needed his social security card to get him into memory care, but I could not find it. Consequently, I went to our local Social Security office to obtain a replacement card for Dad. While there I learned a hard lesson; they don't recognize POA. POA gave me the authority to buy a new home for my parents, facilitate the sale of their old one, and write checks to pay their bills, but evidently it is not accepted for something simple like a replacement government card. I understand that there are rules for a reason, but this was a little frustrating and frankly made no sense to me. But what could I do? I prayed that this would work out.

The SSA office did furnish me with a form for Dad to sign. Perhaps it was just my perspective but I didn't think that the clerk was overly empathetic when I explained that Dad has cognitive issues and was in a Virginia hospital. Truthfully, I wasn't sure if he could sign the form. Plus, Mom wasn't here to represent him. The clerk was unfazed; if he didn't sign the form, her hands were tied. Once again, as a follower of Christ I tried to exhibit grace to the employee; I imagine that they often deal with angry customers, and I didn't need to follow suit.

I left the office and subsequently e-mailed the form to Diane in Virginia. Thankfully she got Dad to sign it at the hospital. I don't think that he understood what he was doing, but we got that part done which was a blessing. Now I needed to find time to get the form back to the Social Security office.

On the 26th, I headed back to Virginia very early in the morning. The previous week I had contacted a number of Dad's friends at local banks, restaurants, and places he patronized. Dad was known, loved, and respected in the community where he and Mom spent the past thirty years. I thought it would be nice if people he knew would write a note of encouragement in greeting cards which I would present to him when he arrived at memory care. The response was overwhelming and brought me (and Diane) to tears with the memories people shared. The supervisor at a local bank shared how grateful she was that Dad taught her son how to drive. Dad was a driver's Ed teacher for years in Virginia and touched the lives of many high school students. He had a light-hearted method of teaching the kids and they never forgot it.

Dad made a difference in many lives and his example encourages me to this day.

On the way home, Diane and I stopped at a Social Security office about forty minutes from Mom and Dad's house in Virginia. That experience could not have been better. The clerk was a Christian woman who graciously processed Dad's signed form. She had the replacement card sent directly to the memory care facility. That issue was solved, praise God! It's amazing how people who are kind and compassionate can encourage you, just when you need it! It is contagious!

Here is a postscript to the "missing social security card" saga, another true story that you just can't make up: After Dad passed in September of 2023, I was gathering records to ensure that Mom received his survivor benefits. I located a file-folder labelled, "Social Security – Bob" buried in a dusty box. Can you guess what I discovered, laminated and taped to the inside back of the folder? You guessed it: Dad's original Social Security card! That was just like Dad in his prime; he was meticulous and organized. I just didn't know where to look!

As I finished this chapter, I went back to my second book, *Family Love Letters*, and read the letter Mom wrote to Diane back in 1983. Diane and I had just started dating and were living and working in Texas. Mom had never met Diane but wrote the sweetest words about me in that letter. I also came across a card Mom had written to Diane's late parents in 1989, right after Mom had surgery for colon cancer. We had just moved to Pennsylvania and Diane spent several days with Mom as she recuperated. Here is what Mom wrote: "I'd like to take this time at Thanksgiving to tell you what a wonderful daughter you have. Diane has unselfishly given so much of herself, especially in my time of need. I just wanted to say 'thank you' for Diane."

I believe that Mom's true self, who she really is, is reflected in the foregoing writings. Moreover, her love is further exhibited in the fact that she took the time to intentionally write those kind words. Ironically, she was still living in New Jersey and seemed to be happy. While it breaks my heart to see things how they are now, I take comfort in memories of better times. Thank God that I have these mementos to look back on.

I prayed that Mom's life would be better in a smaller home, near family, with better medical care and community. But in the back of my mind, I knew that nothing would measure up to her perceived life in Virginia.

Chapter 14: Dad's Release

Now the Lord is the Spirit, and where the Spirit of the Lord is, there is freedom.

2 Corinthians 3:17

The 31st of January, 2023 was a day that had been on my mind since December of 2022. For what seemed like an eternity, I had concerns about Dad being released from the hospital too soon, never being released at all, guilt over having him there in the first place, and a waiting list to get into assisted living near me. And now all of that was coming to an end. The hospital, memory care facility, and the judicial system coordinated and agreed on this release date.

My brother graciously offered to drive down from New Jersey and pick Dad up from the hospital in Virginia. He would transport Dad to the memory care facility in

Pennsylvania where Diane and I would be waiting. I was anxious, not knowing how Dad would handle the five-hour drive, after being isolated in a hospital for forty days. He was moving from a place where he had little freedom to a place where he would at least have some independence. He would also receive specialized care which would ultimately save and extend his life, in my opinion.

Back in Virginia, Dad's friend Norman drove Mom to the hospital to see Dad off. From what I understand and can only imagine, it was a tearful and emotional goodbye. From this point, Mom was alone in Virginia. She became desperate to sell her home and move and be near Dad. She continually texted that she wanted to immediately move from Virginia to be with him. I was doing my best to make that happen as quickly as possible.

Sadly, Mom does not recall the foregoing reality today and often asserts that she could and should have stayed on the "farm." Even the casual observer would agree that this was not a possibility, especially with what was to come with her physical health. It saddens me when I think about the fact that Dad would never return to his Virginia home again. He truly never got closure on leaving the place he loved. However, in his state of mind then until the day he died, I don't believe that Dad ever looked back.

My brother enjoyed a rich time talking with Dad on the long ride from Virginia to Pennsylvania. He brought a cooler full of soft drinks and snacks for Dad to enjoy along the way. I was in the office of the assisted living facility finalizing paperwork when my brother and Dad walked in. Dad seemed out of sorts, but I was very happy to see him. Diane was over in the secure memory care building, getting Dad's room ready for him. She hung pictures of family and decorated the room with memorabilia familiar to Dad.

We were only able to get Dad admitted on the 31st because a bed in a double room became available, meaning that he would have a roommate. As we entered the memory care unit, Dad said, "I'm probably going to die here so can I at least have a single room?" I was astonished at Dad's awareness and comment but promised to get him a single as soon as there was an opening. It would take several weeks but he did finally get his own room. We showed Dad the stack of cards from friends in Virginia who had sent their well-wishes, but he was overwhelmed; I don't know that he fully appreciated the sentiments and just how loved he was.

I felt like things were finally coming together. Step one had been completed: getting Dad here safely. I was now laser-focused on step two: selling the Virginia property and moving Mom. This latter step would be no easy feat. My parents had so much "stuff," not to mention three horses and three donkeys who would need homes, as well as two cats who needed to be transported to Pennsylvania.

But something unexpected and distressing was about to happen. There aren't enough platitudes to describe it. "You can't make this stuff up, when it rains it pours…" If it were just Dad…

Chapter 15: Rock Bottom Was Still Below

For though the righteous fall seven times, they rise again, but the wicked stumble when calamity strikes.

Proverbs 24:16

On February 1, 2023, I thanked God in my quiet time for getting Dad into memory care after forty days in a hospital. The transition went remarkably well, all things considered. Mom complained continually because of the cost, but what could we do? This facility is reasonable considering Dad's needs and the cost of comparable facilities. I studied Economics in college and learned on the first day of class that there is no such thing as a "free lunch." Things may be "free" to someone, but someone else always has to pick up the tab when services are provided.

Besides the cost of the room, Dad required a level of care which commanded an additional fee. Elder care, no matter how you slice it, is expensive. I won't get into the multiple ways there are to pay for it but suffice it to say, everyone's needs and resources are different. Since this is such a complex subject, attorneys who specialize in Elder Law are extremely valuable, in my view. They, and trusted financial advisors can provide wisdom and advice on funding options for elder care.

The fact is, Dad was in the best place possible and, while my parents' resources are not unlimited, the cost was sustainable for the time being. We did not have many choices, and I was thankful that the memory care facility admitted him. The staff and leadership were wonderful. They loved and respected my father. Occasionally I run into staff members from the facility when I'm out and about in the community. It blesses me that they fondly remember my dad. I prayed that he would adjust and that Mom would settle down and find peace accepting things as they were.

Being alone in Virginia, all Mom wanted to do now was "move and be with her husband," though she still expressed second thoughts. She would get her wish to move but not before things would go very wrong with her health.

As I mentioned earlier, Mom had issues with her tailbone and spine since 2022, possibly before that. Past physical therapy seemed to help, and she had been relatively mobile. But on this day those issues would take center stage.

Mom would often ask me, "How do you think I injured myself?" Did the past fall in the pasture trigger this? Did the pet hound dog pull her down one too many times? Or was it the result of a heavy box she lifted preparing for the move? Perhaps it was the culmination of years on the farm, hoisting hay bales and feed, and working in the pastures? Or was her age and normal "wear and tear" the issue? All of those factors may have contributed but I don't think we will ever know for sure.

On this fine February day, I planned to visit Dad in memory care when I received an unexpected call from Mom. She was crying and said that she had excruciating back pain. We did not have a caregiver scheduled that day for Mom and I was five hours away. I asked her to call for an ambulance, but she didn't want to do that. Thankfully I got in contact with Norman, Dad's friend who helped take care of their animals and property. Norman drove to Mom's place and took her to the ER in Virginia, about forty-five minutes from her property. He waited with her for hours while she was examined, x-rayed, and consequently prescribed strong medication for pain. From what I understand, Norman had a tough time on the rides to and from the hospital while Mom moaned and screamed in pain. Historically Mom has not handled pain well but back pain is different; most people I know with back issues will tell you that it's the worst kind of pain. My heart and prayers went out to Mom.

To make matters worse, Dad had a terrible day in memory care. He was scared and confused, which is typical when someone is moved into a new facility. It is a big adjustment from what I learned. He was eating and drinking adequately but kept repeating, "I don't know what to do, I'm so scared." I never dreamed that I'd be taking my dad to the bathroom and cleaning him up, because he had no idea what to do himself, but this was one of the things he forgot. I am not a medical professional, so this was all new to me and I felt very inadequate. Thankfully the staff helped me with Dad's subsequent trips to the bathroom. The best way to describe the way I felt was "numb." I now had two parents out of commission, and one was still five hours away...

Mom returned home from the ER, with temporary relief from the strong meds. While her mind was temporarily not focused on her pain, she suggested that we search for a "cheaper" real estate agent, i.e., one who charges a minimal commission. I recommended that we use the agent who originally sold them the land over thirty years ago. He has been a friend to Mom and Dad over the years and was familiar with the property. He was also respected in the area and ran an auction business, which was an added blessing. An auction would help Mom downsize her "stuff." But Mom decided to make some phone calls. With everything I had on my plate I did not need this. I needed "simple, efficient and predictable."

Fortunately, none of the "cheaper" agents returned her calls. We went with the agent I originally recommended and ultimately, he did an amazing job.

Given Mom's back pain, coupled with growing short-term memory issues, the need to move was becoming more urgent. Things were not happening quickly enough for Mom and it was frustrating when she complained. I kept coming back to Dad's example and my commitment to the Lord, and the realization that Mom had a great deal of pain. I prayed for strength. Regardless of what was going on, I could do no less than be there for my parents. Galatians 6:9 in God's Word reminded me that I could not give up.

Dad had not been formally diagnosed with dementia (yet), but the obvious signs were there. I am not a doctor, but it was evident that he had some type of cognitive issue. But make no mistake, Dad was not stupid. I spent a great deal of time with him, and we shared many memories together. He understood more than he could articulate but there was no way to know exactly what was going through his mind. It was heartbreaking to see him in this state, unable to express himself adequately. Dad never forgot who I was, but did sometimes confuse one of my siblings with one of his siblings.

I visited Dad in memory care one morning and reviewed his finances. I showed him my plan for buying the new house and selling the Virginia property. He agreed with it, made a few comments and, yes, comprehended everything

I was saying. Even though he struggled with words and his memory was "patchy," the financial expert I knew still understood.

As a musician I view life through certain "glasses." You might call it perspective or worldview. I believe that our purpose, what motivates us, is tantamount to a song. Thanks to my relationship with Jesus Christ, there are many things that make my heart sing. If you're struggling right now, please stop for a moment and consider: "What makes your heart sing?" At this point in my life, with everything going on, I felt like I had lost most of my song.

I prayed that the Holy Spirit would envelop the memory care facility and fill every employee and resident with the joy and peace that only comes from the Lord. I also prayed that His Holy Spirit would fill Mom and cover that property in Virginia, in Jesus's name. I believe that He answered both of those prayers in His will and perfect timing.

Every day was surreal. One morning I went to visit Dad in memory care. We had a few good moments and then he had a meltdown; emotional, confused, and scared. Later that night I received a call from the facility. They said Dad was inconsolable, saying he was going to die. I tried talking to him on the phone but to no avail. Finally, the nurse came back on and said that our conversation calmed him down. Thank God.

As for Mom, it got to the point where she was literally bedridden in Virginia, on heavy meds. I have to re-emphasize that she was totally immobile and in severe pain. To say that she doesn't remember this period of time, nor our desperate situation would be the understatement of the year. To this day she sometimes laments that she never should have sold her farm and that she could have stayed there. But she could not walk nor take care of herself and she was isolated. Moving to our area and receiving specialized medical care would literally save her life. I prayed that Dad would improve and that Mom could be healed. I prayed that they could see each other at least one more time.

If all of this weren't enough, I had an issue with their tax return from the previous year, requiring hours of research, phone calls, and online work with a past investment firm. Eventually the issue was rectified but I didn't need this on top of everything else. "When it rains it pours" and other platitudes could apply here. I couldn't recall a harder time in my life but thanked the Lord for His past goodness and faithfulness. His strength carried us through this.

It was only February 4th of 2023, not even two months since Dad's incidents in Virginia, and so much had transpired. In my quiet time, I was grateful for the new day but short on words. I spent four hours with Dad in memory care the night before. It was very difficult to see how far he had declined.

Mom was totally incapacitated in Virginia due to severe back and leg pain. She called me during the night crying because her caregiver, who had spent countless hours with Mom, some on her own time, had gone out for an errand and had yet to return. Mom said that she was gone for three hours but in reality, she was gone for less than an hour. I know that Mom was in pain, but her short-term memory was declining. I didn't mean to sound indifferent but I was five hours away. Besides my heart being broken, hearing Mom in such distress, what could I do?

Just being transparent and I've said this at other tough times during this storm: My emotions were fragile and part of me was resentful, knowing that some of this situation was likely avoidable if my parents had not remained in southern Virginia so long. They had the opportunity to move when their health was relatively good, and refused. I prayed that the Lord would soften my heart and work everything out for His glory. I knew I couldn't look back, only forward.

I quickly learned a new term that affects certain people as they age: "sundowning." My layman's understanding is that in the late afternoon/early evening, people with memory issues can become agitated and exhibit behaviors such as confusion, anxiety, and aggression. This happened several times with Dad, and I would eventually see it with Mom as well.

On this night Dad either fell or simply laid down on the floor in memory care. Once again, he told the staff that he was dying. Based on the fact that he was not injured I believe that the latter was the case, i.e., he laid down on the floor. Anytime something like this happened I received a phone call. My phone rang often.

At some point a doctor prescribed an anti-anxiety agent to calm Dad down in extreme cases, and that med was used this night to stabilize him. The staff at the facility was always compassionate, professional, empathetic, and totally on top of things. They kept me informed of everything and I will always be grateful for that! Dad was in the best place, given his condition. I often had to overlook his words and behavior and realize that he had a disease. His cognition continued to decline.

And the day would not have been complete if Mom had not gone to the ER in Virginia, again! This time her caregiver drove Mom to the hospital when she was in excruciating pain. Thank God for her caregivers. I was so unsure of the end game and could not foresee a happy ending in this storm. I prayed that Mom would be healed and could physically make the move to Pennsylvania, close to Dad, and her family.

Chapter 16: Another Unplanned Blessing

Come, let us sing for joy to the Lord; let us shout aloud to the Rock of our salvation. Let us come before Him with thanksgiving and extol Him with music and song.

Psalm 95:1-2

t was February 6th. I was thankful to attend both Sunday school and our church service. It had been a while and I was grateful for something "normal." Diane and I drove straight from church to visit Dad in memory care. I brought my guitar along, hoping that he might enjoy some calming music and singing. I walked into Dad's room and Diane remained behind to chat with a staff member she knows. I think I had played one song for Dad and his roommate when Diane came into the room. She interrupted and said, "The staff saw you carrying your guitar and asked if you would play for the residents?" "Where?" I asked. Diane said, "In the dining room." "When?" I asked. "Right now…" I reluctantly agreed but had no idea what I would play (and sing). I was not prepared for an audience but was happy to serve in any way I could. I also sensed that perhaps God was up to something. Psalm 37:4 says, "Take delight in the Lord, and He will give you the desires of your heart." My Lord and Savior was about to bless me with a long-standing desire of my heart.

Ironically, back in 2020 when I retired from my second career, I planned to prepare a repertoire of songs and offer to play and sing at nursing homes and senior facilities. I felt like God was calling me to do this and I was excited about pursuing this ministry. Then Covid hit. And then Dad's health deteriorated. The opportunity was lost for the time being, perhaps forever, and I had forgotten about it.

I obviously had nothing prepared musically but walked into the dining room where a few people sat. I was surprised but so blessed at what happened next: people kept on coming, some under their own power, some via wheelchair, others by walker. And soon the room was full. Actually, it was beyond full.

Music has been such a big part of my life and has seen me through a lot of hard times. Even during the years before Christ, when I played professionally and practiced a sinful lifestyle, God used that time to prepare me musically. Ultimately, He equipped me to play in churches and serve as a worship leader. Nothing is ever wasted with our Lord; He can use anything for His glory.

I have several songs I can play off the top of my head, so I started with a few familiar hymns. Some additional standard and popular songs came to mind, and I played and sang those. As I was singing, I got choked up by the reactions of these dear residents. My understanding is that a number of patients were not vocal. However, I observed firsthand how music can have an amazing effect on people. Many were singing, clapping, humming along, and tapping their feet, with lots of smiles. Dad was one of them. At one point he blurted out, "This is my son!" It was hard not to shed a few tears.

When I couldn't think of what to sing next, staff members requested songs. I probably played for an hour and a half. Holding back tears I thanked God for this opportunity. As I continued to play and sing, I thought, "This is what I wanted to do three years ago. I was not prepared and never dreamed I'd be doing this." And yet here I was. Praise the Lord! In the midst of this storm, I experienced great joy and love for these dear residents. All in His perfect timing. All for His glory!

I praised God for this unexpected blessing. I am amazed and grateful how God works all things for our good. Jumping ahead for a moment to 2024, God has opened up opportunities to play and sing in the local senior center where I take Mom from time-to-time for socialization and encouragement.

Interacting with and ministering to these dear senior friends has become one of my greatest privileges and joy. And God continues to open other doors for music ministry. Based on what has happened in this storm, the blessings from these music opportunities are sweeter than I could have imagined. Ironically, if Dad and Mom had not experienced their health issues, I never would have encountered these opportunities nor the wonderful people I've met. He gave me the desires of my heart, not as or when I expected them, but in His perfect timing. And He continues to do that...

Chapter 17: Back to Reality

This is what we speak, not in words taught us by human wisdom but in words taught by the Spirit, explaining spiritual realities with Spirit-taught words.

1 Corinthians 2:13

The mountaintop experience was short-lived and it was quickly "back to business." Mom's pain and memory issues would now take center stage. I headed back to Virginia on February 8th. I am not a medical professional nor caregiver but would be thrusted into a role I was completely unprepared for. I prayed that I would have the strength and wisdom to deal with what I was about to face. And what I was about to face continues to consume a significant part of my life to this current day (as I'm writing this). Today we have 24/7 in-home care for Mom, which provides a safety net for Diane and me, but we'll talk more about that a little later…

Mom was in excruciating pain when I arrived at the house. She calmed down a little as the day went on and said that she had less pain, but she was immobile and needed supervision. Often, she felt better during daylight hours, mainly because she could be repositioned, but was still a serious fall risk. While I was there, the real estate agent stopped by and Mom signed the contract to sell the Virginia property. I had not met the buyers since I was not there when the house was shown, so I had no idea who they were. Since Dad was now in Pennsylvania, I signed for him as POA based on his and Mom's wishes. I had conferred with him a number of times about the plans to sell the house and he was completely on board. All he wanted was to see his wife.

Whenever I believed that things were turning a corner, something usually happened. Mom could not walk or even dress herself. She would wake up during the night, writhing and screaming in pain. It was heartbreaking to see her this way. One morning she woke up with chest pain and, unbeknownst to me, had taken two nitro pills. Mom has a heart condition, and her cardiologist had prescribed nitroglycerine to be taken as needed for mild chest pain. In this case she had taken one too many!

I went in to check on her and she stated that she had a splitting headache. The fact that she had taken two pills, and I found another on the floor, told me that she was not in her right mind. Since she couldn't walk on her own, I had to help her to the bathroom. On the way, she went limp in my arms and collapsed. Thank God that I was holding onto her so that when she began to fall, I was able to gently lay her down on the bedroom floor. Had I not been there my mother likely would not have survived the incident.

At first, she was not responsive, so I wasn't sure if it was a heart attack, a fainting spell, or worse. I was panicked, numb, and fearful at the same time. I immediately called 911. While I was talking to the dispatcher, Mom regained consciousness but was not coherent. I waited for the medics to arrive and was able to get her to the bathroom, and then back into bed. I must say that, though they service a rural area, the medics and first responders got to the house quickly. I was impressed with their expertise and compassion and how they treated Mom. I was also grateful for how calm they made me feel as I'm sure my heart rate was elevated.

Mom's heart condition, blood pressure, and level of pain concerned the medics. They checked her vitals and suspected that Mom had experienced Orthostatic hypotension where blood pressure suddenly drops drastically. Mom did not want to go to the hospital and the medics could not force her, but they articulated their concerns. I pleaded with Mom to go; with all that was going on with her health I was hoping that she could be admitted, diagnosed, and treated. Interestingly, the medics would not transport Mom based on my pleading—

they needed to hear it from her. Thankfully, she finally agreed to go. However, she wanted to be cleaned up and dressed first.

A new caretaker was scheduled to come to the house that morning. She showed up as the medics were talking to Mom. This woman had never met Mom but was so sweet and empathetic. She immediately stepped in and started caring for Mom. The caretaker bathed Mom before the ambulance transported her to the hospital. The medics were patient, kind, and understanding. On my way out the door I met the caregiver's husband, who had driven his wife to my parents' house. He is a pastor and we hit it off immediately. When I explained what was going on with Mom, he prayed with me. Another God-orchestrated moment, and just what I needed at the right time.

I followed the ambulance on the forty-five-minute ride to the hospital. Unfortunately, the ER was full so the medics met me in the hospital parking lot. They invited me to sit in the ambulance with Mom until a room opened up. One of the medics asked me if Mom had a habit of repeating herself. I was not aware of this development but started to notice when this behavior became prominent. In the ambulance, Mom was stable and I texted a picture of her to my siblings. Mom was smiling, giving the "thumbs up" in the photo. She was in much better spirits than she had been at home. Of course, that would all change. It always does...

I spent all day in the ER with Mom, awaiting various tests and results. I hadn't eaten since early morning so was not in the best spirits. I became "hangry" as they say. The doctor gave Mom a prescription for new pain meds but those only provided temporary relief. Even before we left the hospital, she was crying and moaning in pain, which radiated from her back, down her right leg. I hated to see my mother in such pain, but I didn't know where to turn. The hospital would not admit her, despite my pleading, and referred us back to her orthopedic doctor in Lynchburg. It would take a while before we could get a telemedicine appointment with him.

Mom could not walk nor care for herself. She was, in essence, bedridden. The drive back to Mom's home was miserable as she cried and screamed in pain. I dreaded the evening because I knew what was coming. I felt helpless and couldn't take much more.

My brother arrived the next day to give me some temporary relief. We went out to lunch and had a great time catching up while the caregiver stayed with Mom. A nurse came and assessed Mom for in-home Physical and Occupational Therapy. I was encouraged that perhaps there was some hope to relieve her pain. My new pastor friend called to check in and prayed over the phone with Mom and me.

Back home, in memory care, Dad was having some back pain himself but thankfully an x-ray and bloodwork didn't reveal any issues. He was sitting a lot which could have caused his pain. Diane had a good visit with him, though Dad was confused and also had episodes of incontinence, which would increase over time.

Since my brother was with Mom, I left her house in the afternoon and spent the night at a hotel, about twenty miles from Mom's place, getting some much-needed sleep. I planned to head home in the morning from there. There had been no rest for me at the house as Mom was up several times a night, moaning and screaming in pain. When I checked my phone at 6:42 am on February 10th, I noticed a missed call from my brother at 12:35 am. I knew that this couldn't be good.

He left a message stating that Mom was in severe pain during the night and he had to call 911. I called my brother who was driving Mom from the hospital back to her house. He had spent the overnight hours in the ER with Mom (if you're counting, that's four visits in a very short timeframe). My brother was a medic at one time so has experience in this area, but he admitted that dealing with Mom's pain was difficult. A formal diagnosis would come from the orthopedic doctor later, but it was the same pattern in the ER; new meds for pain and Mom was sent home. I felt guilty leaving my brother there while I went home. I knew that I would be back shortly and staying for a while.

It was difficult, and most times, not even possible to get Mom a caregiver for twenty-four consecutive hours. I was on the phone continually with the agency, which worked tirelessly to provide coverage, but it was spotty at best based on caregiver availability. It would have been very expensive to have the care 24/7 and I would have paid for it, but it simply wasn't available. However, that is what we needed. Mom absolutely could not be left alone. Occupational therapists surmised that she may never walk again. It was always stressful during the time slots when I couldn't get in-home care for Mom. I continued to pray. At times it seemed like God was silent even though I knew He heard my prayers. How long, Lord?

My brother could not remain in Virginia for long so I was basically home for a day and headed right back to Mom's. I predicted that I would be staying until their house was sold and closing occurred on the property. I couldn't leave Mom alone but didn't know how I would provide the level of care she needed. I also dreaded the nights and wondered how I would endure her pain episodes.

Mom was in good spirits when I arrived back at her place. Sometimes during the day, she would be sitting up in bed with breakfast and coffee (prepared by her caregiver or me) and say, "I feel great." One morning when a caregiver was on-site Mom said, "There's my son, he takes such good care of me." I hate to admit this but, after a while, I would roll my eyes at those words because at night, when the pain hit, she would become a totally different person. Dr. Jekyll became Mr. Hyde and I went from "saint" to "devil" when there was nothing I could do to relieve her pain.

One physical therapist had told my brother that Mom may have suffered a mini-stroke based on her behavior and neuropathy in her right foot. I continually prayed that she would be pain-free and could possibly get a spinal injection for relief. I coordinated with the orthopedic doctor via on-line portal and learned that there was a long wait time for the injection. Moreover, the procedure would need to be done at a facility which was an hour and a half from Mom's home. There was a shorter wait time if Mom had the injection in the doctor's office, also in Lynchburg, but there would be no anesthesia. This was a major concern for me because of Mom's low tolerance for pain.

On February 12th I wrote:

In VA, raining. I feel like I'm living in a nightmare. Mom had some good moments yesterday but then the very painful ones. Kaye (Caregiver) is a saint but left at 8:30 last night. Mom had me up at 3:00 a.m. and then 5:45 with excruciating pain. I gave her prescription med and Tylenol at 3:00 but can't give another pill until 9:00. How long, Lord? I'm so tired and she's no better. She can't walk and is bedridden. Please give us hope, Lord.

Diane and I were tag-teaming, caring for both of my parents. While I was in Virginia with Mom, Diane visited Dad in memory care back in Pennsylvania. He continued to go downhill. One parent with severe health issues was bad enough. Two parents down coupled with this five-hour drive was too much to bear. I am not an experienced caregiver, and this was way more than I could handle. If it were just Dad...

Walking around the Virginia house, seeing Dad's empty chair and office, missing who he was, it was so hard. I realized that I had been mourning him for a long time. Even though he was still alive, in a real sense, I lost him several years ago.

I had survived two nights alone with Mom. On a "good" night she had me up at 10:45 p.m. and then 5:00 a.m. when I had to take her to the bathroom. Her pain could be manageable and then flare up at a moment's notice.

We had a caregiver on a Sunday morning, so I was able to attend a local church with a friend of my parents'. The lesson that morning from 2 Corinthians 1 spoke to me and was just what I needed to hear. I walked out of church knowing that He is the God of all comfort and would see me through this storm. But it was still difficult.

In-home physical therapy helped to get Mom walking a little bit, with assistance. One afternoon Mom was feeling "better" so I took her and her caregiver out for milkshakes. Kaye and I had to pretty much carry Mom down the steps from the front door to my vehicle. Of course, whenever Mom felt "better" she would repeat phrases like, "See, I am fine and can live on my own." That pattern continues, although to a lesser extent, to this day.

Then dinnertime rolled around, and the pain came back with a vengeance. She was moaning when the caregiver left and screaming by 11:45 p.m. Nothing I did helped her. I gave her a pain pill, but she was still unreasonable, inconsolable, and in "help me" mode. I need to be honest: I will have PTSD over these memories for the rest of my life. Hearing my mother scream in pain and not being able to provide relief was unbearable. I never want to experience that again.

For the few moments when she did fall asleep, I tried to lay my head down but sleep was impossible. I knew that "it" was coming. I would hear the initial moan, then "somebody help me," then "I'm in pain," and finally, "I need a pill," (the volume increasing to yelling then screaming). This was not like Mom, so the pain had to be excruciating. Once again, I had to dial 911, but, when medics arrived, she was feeling slightly better and refused to go to the hospital. The medics were so patient and became very familiar with travelling to Mom's house. There would be no ER visit but, of course, no sleep for me (again). If not for the Lord's presence and strength in my life, I'm certain that I would have had a breakdown.

Chapter 18: The Diagnoses

Be strong and courageous. Do not be afraid or terrified
because of them, for the Lord your God goes with you; He will
never leave you nor forsake you.

Deuteronomy 31:6

While I was still in Virginia dealing with Mom, Dad had a telemedicine call with the psychiatrist who services the memory care facility in Pennsylvania. I was grateful for the leadership at the facility. They were able to accelerate his scheduled appointment based on the seriousness of Dad's condition. Diane was there with Dad. Mom and I connected from Virginia via my computer. We listened as the doctor compassionately asked Dad questions and got to know him. The doctor had done his homework and knew Dad's history—intimately. At the conclusion of the appointment Dad finally had a diagnosis: vascular dementia with depression. It was the first time I heard this from a doctor, but I was not surprised.

Dad's dementia was likely advanced by his two strokes. In the past there wasn't much the medical profession could do for the disease. The sad fact is that it is an incurable disease which affects the brain. Ultimately, Dad would succumb to it. But there are medicines and treatments which can make life bearable and even better for the patient. Dad was prescribed meds to help with his paranoia and depression. Over the next several weeks we would see some improvement—for a while anyway. Diane refers to this as our "honeymoon period" with Dad. He did better mentally and socially in memory care. At one point, leadership even considered possibly moving Dad to the assisted living side. However, Dad never quite got to the point where that could occur. In my opinion, the doctor and the facility added months to Dad's life. I am eternally grateful to the Lord for this and so much more.

After that session, Mom and I had a telemedicine call with the orthopedic doctor in Virginia. Mom was immobile so she sat up in bed as we talked with the doctor. I had taken Mom to see him in late 2022 when her back was bothering her. The trip was always an ordeal as the office was approximately ninety minutes away from her home. Based on that visit, previous X-rays and MRIs, and the four ER visits, she now had a diagnosis and it wasn't good. Mom was suffering from numerous back issues including a bulging lumbar disc, sciatica, spinal stenosis and degenerative disc disease. She also had a fractured tailbone as well as neuropathy in her right foot. All of this explained her pain and lack of mobility.

Based on those conditions, her age, and other factors, the options going forward were few. Her back condition and spinal stenosis causes pain to radiate from her back down to her feet. Additionally, she has constant pain in the tailbone area. As time progressed, additional related issues would be diagnosed. For now, we needed to figure out how to manage Mom's pain because the status quo wasn't working for anyone.

The doctor prescribed another opioid for pain and increased one of her existing meds to reduce inflammation. All of that made little difference; that night she had me up with her usual cadence at 10:30, 12:30, 2:00, 3:00, and 4:00 a.m. I was so sleep-deprived that I was becoming depressed and delirious, very close to a nervous breakdown. I felt so bad about her pain, but this was difficult for me as well. Like many others, when I am tired it affects my perspective and behavior. I was exhausted.

The pattern started with the familiar moaning, "the pain, help me…" and just got louder. These words and sounds will haunt me for life. I would try to comfort her with soothing words or by repositioning her in the bed, but to no avail. Also, she could only take so many pills in prescribed timeframes. When she begged for more and I couldn't give them, she would yell and scream. This was so unlike my mom.

I can't imagine the pain she was going through and my heart went out to her.

Mom had a number of pain pills and muscle relaxers prescribed by different ER doctors. I had to be very careful administering these powerful drugs. One night during a pain episode, when she begged for a pill, I researched possible drug interactions out of concern. Thank God I didn't give Mom a muscle relaxer with the pain med she was taking. It could have been fatal. I sent a text to a nurse who had visited Mom in the past. She checked the same website I did and confirmed that I did the right thing.

The orthopedic doctor was to schedule her for an epidural shot but based on availability, it had to be done in the office, meaning only local anesthetic. The procedure in a hospital, where she could be sedated, was booked months into the future. I prayed that she could get the injection and be relieved from the pain. The only other option appeared to be complex, painful surgery. At Mom's age and with her tolerance for pain, this was a last resort. Moreover, due to multiple issues with her back, risks, recovery time, rehab and other health issues, surgery likely would be pointless.

These days when I remind Mom of all that transpired in Virginia, she remembers very little. She attributes this to her level of pain, the trauma of moving, and even Covid. Some of that may be true but it was clear to me that something bigger was also going on with her memory and her behavior. We would get a diagnosis for that later.

I had planned to remain with Mom for the long haul, but I was extremely sleep-deprived. Out of desperation I asked my sister if she would come down to relieve me for a few days. I was thankful that she agreed to drive down and stay with Mom for a short time. That night, before my sister arrived, Mom was in agony again. The pain radiated from her back down her leg. The caregiver encouraged me to call the orthopedist to see if Mom could get an appointment soon for the spinal injection. I was grateful for this suggestion and thankful that the doctor had availability on the upcoming Friday. My sister and the caregiver would take Mom on the hour and a half drive for the shot. I prayed that the injection would give Mom the relief she needed. My sister showed up at about 10:30 that night and I was able to sleep before heading home the following morning.

Back home I visited Dad who was struggling at first, but I left on a good note. Over the next several days his demeanor would improve, no doubt due to the new meds and prayer. Physical and occupational therapy at the facility also helped to stabilize him. I had so much financial and administrative work to do for the impending move and sale of their Virginia property. At least I was able to get a couple nights of sleep in my own bed.

On Friday of that week my sister and the caregiver took Mom to the orthopedist's office for the scheduled injection. However, Mom could not tolerate the pain during the injection and her screams were heard throughout the facility. I'm thankful that I wasn't there! The doctor had to cut the procedure short but still hoped that the shot would be somewhat effective. Mom experienced slight relief for a few days but then things would quickly go downhill again. In essence, the injection did nothing for her. Now what?

Subsequently my brother visited Mom for a few days. While he was there, I drove Diane to my oldest daughter's place in northern Virginia. The plan was that my daughter would drive Diane down to southern Virginia to help Mom with her health and organize things for the upcoming move. It would also be a good opportunity for my daughter to visit Mom and to see my brother.

I got the impression from my brother that Mom was angry with me due to the situation she was in. I kept reviewing the events of the last couple years with Mom, reminding myself of the truth and reality of her circumstances. I'd done my best to fulfill their wishes and had no control over her or Dad's medical conditions. I also had to remind myself that I didn't cause all of this and was doing exactly what they asked me to do, especially what Dad wanted.

I continued to take solace in the knowledge that this is how Dad would have handled things if he were in his right mind. I was overwhelmed but prayed that I could get everything done that needed to be done.

I was very concerned about Mom's health and the fact that she was alone during times when Diane and I couldn't be there. Caregivers provided support but, again, availability was an issue; we simply couldn't get them 24/7. I didn't know what to do. I fashioned my life to be simple and organized. Now my parents' issues had become mine. But God had a reason for me being in this position and provided the strength I need to do His will. His Word reminds me that His ways are much higher than mine and that there is purpose in trials, including this one.

For now, I was at home and Diane was in Virginia. Mom still struggled with back pain at night and unreasonable talk and behavior in the day. Evidently Mom got very upset with Diane when she refused to give Mom a pill. Again, the pills had to be given at prescribed intervals to preclude an overdose. Mom didn't realize that both Diane and I were protecting her from potentially fatal overdoses or drug interactions.

At one point Diane recorded one of Mom's pain episodes where she screamed and cried out in pain. With Mom's permission Diane played the recording for Dr. H, Mom's primary care physician. The doctor's jaw dropped when she heard Mom's screams. She had never seen anything like it. Besides feeling bad for Mom, the good doctor expressed sympathy for Diane and me as well.

Back in Pennsylvania, Dad was doing remarkably well. He still struggled with words and short-term memory, but he was more stable and no longer paranoid. He wasn't "happy," but he wasn't unhappy either. On February 22nd I signed Dad out of memory care for a few hours and took him to lunch at a local restaurant. He loved the food and being out of the facility. I was grateful for how well he was doing. I continued to pray for Mom; mentally and physically she was not well. I was thankful to have secured home-care coverage for the rest of the week after Diane was scheduled to come home from Virginia.

It was back to Virginia on the 23rd. Mom was not doing well. She was noticeably forgetful and repeated herself constantly. Diane got a lot done there in preparation for selling their house. I picked Diane up and we brought one of Mom's cats back to Pennsylvania. "White" is a feral cat that showed up at Mom and Dad's door years ago. Dad actually saved his life; the poor cat had gotten his head stuck in an aluminum can and Dad gave the feline its freedom. White would get into fights with other cats, often on the losing end. Eventually Dad brought him in, and he has been a housecat ever since. White has his share of battle scars but is so sweet. We have no idea how old he is.

The cat spent his days in Dad's office. Dad trained White to give him a "head bump" where the cat would gently touch his forehead to Dad's. He was Dad's special buddy and now enjoys his life in Pennsylvania. I visit White almost every day and try to show him the same love Dad exhibited. In Dad's honor, when I say, "White, give me a head bump," the cat presses his head against my forehead.

It was an interesting trip home. We were on the road for about twenty-five minutes when White decided to leave a deposit in the back of our vehicle. We wouldn't have known until the smell gave it away. We were on a rural road but had to pull over to alleviate the odor. We are not litterbugs but somewhere in the brush down there lies a scrunched-up paper towel with ... well, you know ...

Until this year I had never made a ten-hour round trip to Mom and Dad's on the same day, but I would do it several times in 2023. After driving down and picking Diane up at Mom's, we arrived home at 10:00 p.m. that night. The cat would be in a room in our basement until we settled on the new house in Pennsylvania. We had two cats of our own at the time, who would not integrate well with my parents' cat, especially since "White" has claws. He seemed happy in the basement as I would feed, water, and brush him every day. Without Dad in Virginia, the cat had not gotten a lot of attention, so he was loving it here.

Jumping ahead for a moment, I was devastated to lose one of our precious cats in August of 2024. Ginger was sleeping on my lap, a place she loved to be, and had a sudden heart attack. She died in my arms. Sorry if you're not a "cat person" or animal lover but she was family to me, and it still hurts.

While Dad was doing "better" Mom continued to exhibit mental and physical issues. I was with Dad when he spoke to her on the phone. He wanted her with him in Pennsylvania and sternly told her to do whatever it takes to get here. Since Mom was immobile, we considered the possibility of rehab as an option to get her walking again. She reluctantly agreed to that, in a facility, if we could find one near us. We didn't have a lot of options. Mom could not walk nor care for herself.

Mom agreed to rehab on two conditions: First, if Diane and me would take care of her cats. Done. And second, only if insurance would pay for it. That was going to be a challenge since there are criteria to be met, including a seventy-two-hour hospital stay, before insurance would pay for rehab. If you recall, we could not get a hospital in Virginia to admit Mom. Diane tirelessly researched and called a number of facilities, but either there were no openings or Mom's insurance would not cover the expensive stay.

It was clear that the injection did not help Mom; she continued to be in excruciating pain, making her basically immobile and miserable. We had another telemedicine call with the orthopedic doctor. He concluded, based on the ineffectiveness of the shot, that surgery was Mom's only permanent solution. However, due to the severity of her condition, age, recovery time, and tolerance for pain, the risks of surgery outweighed the rewards. I told the doctor that we were considering rehab in Pennsylvania and he agreed that it was worth trying. Diane miraculously found a place near us, within our budget, which would take Mom. I thank God for a friend who reviewed Mom's reports and was able to accept her at a rehab facility. Of course, there was a wait to be admitted. Nothing was ever easy.

Chapter 19: The Moves

Do you not know? Have you not heard? The Lord is the everlasting God, the Creator of the ends of the earth. He will not grow tired or weary, and His understanding no one can fathom.

Isaiah 40:28

On February 4th we made settlement on the Pennsylvania home and then headed back to Virginia. Looking back, purchasing the home that quickly, given the competitive market and shortage of houses, was a miraculous feat. The real estate agents were incredulous that things could happen this quickly, but God gets the glory! Still, no good deed goes unpunished as we would soon experience.

The plan was to move Mom and some of her household goods and personal items so that she could live in the new place with basic necessities. My brother and his son brought a rented trailer to the Virginia home for that purpose. Diane and I would drive Mom and her second cat, Cricket, back to Pennsylvania. The big move of household goods would come later, in tandem with the sale of the Virginia property.

At this point I had lost about fifteen pounds, was not sleeping, nor taking care of myself. My life was consumed with my parents. Both needed attention and we did our best to be there for them. I am so grateful for my wife and don't know how I would have managed without her love and support. I was hopeful that Mom could make the five-hour trip from southern Virginia to Pennsylvania without pain. I also hoped that she would react well to the new house but, deep in my heart, I knew that she would hate it. Unfortunately, I was right. To this day, nothing compares with the perceived utopia she had in Virginia.

The day didn't start out badly. I had to get one of Mom's prescriptions filled at a pharmacy about twenty-five minutes from her Virginia house. The pharmacist and staff were not having the best day; a nearby chain pharmacy (the one I used for Mom) was closed for two days. Thus, this small pharmacy received some unplanned business, along with some unhappy customers. I ended up praying with them and we mutually encouraged each other. It was a great blessing. Then the rest of the day happened ...

Diane and I packed some things and cleaned Mom's house to the extent we could. She still had so much stuff accumulated in thirty years that subsequent trips would be needed! My brother and his son arrived with the truck and we loaded a few pieces of furniture and basic household goods Mom would need in Pennsylvania. As stated previously, a bigger move with professional movers would come later. Mom was in some pain but in pretty good spirits. But that would all change quickly.

We left the property, and Mom was not as emotional as I thought she would be, perhaps because she was experiencing back pain. Her second cat, Cricket, fussed during the entire trip. The cat was stressed during the five-hour ride and urinated in her carrier. About an hour from the new house in Pennsylvania she got sick all over Diane. I felt bad for the cat and my wife. This was a harbinger of things to come.

It was nighttime when we arrived at the new house. As soon as Mom walked in, she expressed her displeasure with the new place, as predicted. While in Virginia, Mom said that she looked forward to moving to the new place and making new friends. Granted, she bought it sight unseen, but we showed her pictures and disclosed every detail about the house. I understood that this was a big change and all new, but it was still frustrating after the very long trip and tiring day.

The simple one-story house was exactly what she needed but not what she wanted. These days she expresses a few things she likes about the house, such as her bedroom, a new walk-in tub and new sunroom. To me it was a miracle that we were able to buy the place at the time we did. And her new neighbors have been a blessing; many have reached out to her and could not be any nicer.

I have to continually remind myself that Mom has been through a lot. Based on counsel from her doctors and books I've studied, her perspective about certain events from the past will likely not change. Due to the passage of time, right medications, and much prayer, we do experience positive moments. As I've learned throughout this storm, things could change suddenly but I am grateful to God for the memories and laughs we still share with Mom.

Diane had to stay at the new house with Mom 24/7 because she was not mobile and could not be left alone. My wife is a saint for all that she endured. Besides Jesus Christ, she is my rock. Back in 1989, Diane and I relocated from central New Jersey to our current home in Pennsylvania. We were in the middle of that move when my mother had extensive surgery for colon cancer. While I was in Pennsylvania, working, Diane stayed with Mom, meeting her every need and actually carrying her to the bathroom. Diane has treated my mother like her own Mom. Mom remembers little about this and that's okay. We don't do any of this for accolades or "credit." Colossians 3:23-24 sums it up nicely: "Whatever you do, work at it with all your heart, as working for the Lord, not for human masters, since you know that you will receive an inheritance from the Lord as a reward. It is the Lord Christ you are serving."

We could not continue to be twenty-four-hour caregivers and I prayed that rehab would open up soon so that we could get a break. I was sleeping alone at home and Diane was at Mom's, in a small spare bedroom on an uncomfortable air mattress which would deflate during the night. I prayed, "Lord, please help us." Hopefully rehab would give us some relief and get Mom on her feet, but then what? Her mind was going, I'm sure due to stress, pain, and understandably, depression. We could not attend church or live a normal life, between visiting Dad in memory care and dealing with Mom's needs and pain.

I remember praying: "Lord, You have brought so many things together in this storm. Please take us out of it. I know that Your grace is sufficient for me as it was for the apostle Paul but I feel like I'm sinking ..."

My journal entry for February 26th:

Jeremiah 29:11 – "For I know the plans I have for you, declares the Lord, plans to prosper you, plans to give you hope and a future." Thank God for His Scriptures which speak truth and encouragement into my life!

On the 27th of February 2023, the storm continued to rage but there were blessings as well. We brought Dad to the new house, and he got to see Mom for the first time in months. However, Mom was immobile and in constant pain. Diane was Mom's full-time caregiver which was taking its toll on her and me. I prayed that we could get Mom to rehab and get some of our life back. It may sound selfish but I'm just being honest. It was a tough time, especially after all that had transpired in Virginia. Both parents were now just a few minutes away from me, which was a blessing. But that introduced new challenges and there was still much to be done in Virginia and Pennsylvania to sustain Mom and Dad.

I dropped paperwork off at the rehab center close to us in Pennsylvania. They had agreed to review Mom's ER reports from Virginia to see if she would qualify for admission. Thankfully they would have a bed available and admit Mom but there was a short wait to get in. I prayed that Mom would be admitted and give the process a chance. I also prayed that this would give Diane a break from the 24/7 care and hopefully "fix" Mom.

I needed to get back to Virginia to sell Mom and Dad's vehicles. Since neither of them could drive any longer, they agreed that it was best to sell the truck and the car. Health care was becoming expensive and the funds from the sale would help. If it were up to me, I would have kept one of the vehicles in the family, but Mom instructed me to sell them. Dad was also on board with the plan so I carried out my parents' wishes.

I was blessed to find a dealer who agreed to purchase both the car and truck. Their Subaru was unreliable as it had a known issue where the battery would drain and need to be recharged. I had the battery replaced with a new one, but it died after only a day. Norman, Dad's good friend and handyman, had to charge the battery to get the car to run. I disclosed this fact to the dealer who thankfully gave us a good price for the car anyway.

Logistically I needed to get the car, the truck and myself to Lynchburg to complete the sale. Thank God for Norman; he and his aunt drove the vehicles from my parents' Virginia property up to Lynchburg. I was able to drive my vehicle from Pennsylvania and meet them at the dealership. It worked out great. I signed the paperwork to complete the sale and subsequently drove Norman and his aunt back to my parents' place in Virginia where their vehicle was parked. Along the way I returned the license plates to the DMV. After Norman and his aunt left, I picked up a few more things from Mom and Dad's house and headed home.

In the middle of the night, I had this conversation with God: "Lord, You brought something to my attention overnight as I woke up at 1 a.m., something I've been doing. While this storm has been long and difficult, I have allowed the circumstances, Mom's condition, Dad's health, and family stuff, to drag me down. I've become cynical, silently complaining, and feeling sorry for myself. That is not who I am in You. I died to those things. Please forgive me and help me handle things one at a time. Thank You dear Lord. Thank You for friends who have come to visit Dad in memory care."

My parents' health issues, expenses and how to pay for them, and all of the unknowns were weighing me down. Yet my hope was in the Lord. I prayed that we could do this financially. I prayed that Mom would get well and walk again.

Mom was finally admitted to rehab at the beginning of March. All my life she made me promise never to put her in a nursing home. While this rehab center is connected to a skilled-care facility, it is not a nursing home per se. Still, she viewed it that way. She evidently had a meltdown several times in the late afternoon (I learned a lot about "sundowning" from dealing with Dad) and now I was getting calls from the rehab center in addition to calls from memory care for Dad. My phone was working overtime.

One night, I was sound asleep, resting in preparation to head back to Virginia at about 4:30 a.m. for the big move of household goods. Sometime around 1:30 a.m. my home phone rang. I knew that something serious was going on because it was the middle of the night, and we rarely use that phone; I always provide my cell number to people for contact information. We have audible caller ID which indicated that the incoming call was from the local hospital. Evidently the hospital tried my cell and, of course, I didn't hear it due to the late hour.

My first thought was, "Mom went off the ranch at the rehab facility." I picked up the phone, half awake, and the voice on the other end identified himself as a nurse from the hospital. It was about Dad; he had fallen in memory care. The nice man said that Dad was very wobbly and was transported to the ER by ambulance. His injury required two staples in the back of his head. He also had a laceration on his leg from the fall. The nurse asked some questions about Dad, including insurance information. I asked if Dad needed to be picked up and the man said that the memory care facility would take care of it. Since I had to leave for Virginia in a few hours I tried to fall back to sleep. That lasted less than an hour...

The ER called again and said that Dad was very upset; no one from the memory care facility was available to pick him up. So, I quickly threw some clothes on and out I went to the hospital, barely awake. It was about thirty degrees outside. When I arrived at the hospital, Dad had only underwear and a T-shirt on. The ER provided a blanket, but Dad was cold and shivering (I had a coat on and was cold myself). Lesson learned: keep spare clothes on-hand for emergencies if your loved one is in assisted living or memory care. It was between 4:00 and 4:30 a.m. when Dad and I arrived back at the memory care facility.

I left Dad in my vehicle, with the heat blasting, and rang the bell to be admitted to the building. I not only needed to get Dad back to his room safely but would need a wheelchair to do it; he was very unsteady on his feet and unable to walk. I waited for several minutes and could not get anyone to answer the bell. At that time of night there was minimal staff, so it was understandable. I finally had to call the main number for the assisted living facility, and someone then came with a wheelchair to help me. Once Dad was safely in his room, I told him to get some rest, and I left. With Dad there and Mom in the rehab facility about fifteen miles from him, I prayed that they would be okay as Diane and I headed to Virginia to facilitate the "big move."

It was March 3, 2023. Although we left early, Diane and I didn't arrive at Mom and Dad's property until about 1:30 in the afternoon. Before that, I had to stop and withdraw money at a local bank for the movers and at the accountant's office to finalize my parents' tax returns. There was never a dull moment. Back home Mom seemed to have a good day in rehab and physical therapy was helping with her pain and mobility. Friends from my Sunday school class also visited Mom which was a blessing to us and her. She had been very isolated in Virginia, and I was thankful that so many here were reaching out to her. I didn't talk to Dad but understand that he had a rough day after his fall.

On March 4th, the professional movers showed up at the Virginia property. Three men and a big truck! They spent several hours packing and loading the mostly large items onto the truck. We spent the day directing them to items which would be moved, keeping separate the things which would be auctioned or transported later by me. Diane and my brother had done a great job placing colored stickers on items to indicate "Move," "Auction," or "Leave alone" (meaning we would haul those items ourselves). The sorting and organizing of Mom's household goods was all done under her supervision. Unfortunately, with her pain and memory issues she recalls very little from this time.

We got the house pretty well cleaned out except for things to be auctioned and small, personal items which we would need to take later. We did not arrive back at our home until after 10:00 that night. The movers would deliver the goods to the new Pennsylvania house the following day, which was Sunday. We were exhausted but couldn't rest for long.

Mom seemed to be doing better in rehab, and I praised God for that. Friends from church visited, though she sometimes forgot who they were. Dad was a little "off." I prayed about the unknown future. God had brought us this far and I had a deep-rooted confidence that He would deliver us out of this storm. But storms are still unnerving when you're in the midst of them.

The delivery of household items to the Pennsylvania home went more quickly than the packing and loading had gone in Virginia. However, we now had a mess on our hands as boxes and furniture covered rooms in the new house as well as the garage. The new house is much smaller than the one in

Virginia and has less storage space. There was so much to do to get the new home in a livable condition.

Both Mom and Dad wanted to come "home." We knew that Mom would come home at some point, hopefully walking and no longer in excruciating pain. I feared that we would be expected to be 24/7 caregivers, and we just could not continue in that role. The trips to Virginia and everything that occurred there had taken its toll on us. I prayed that God would make a way for us and, as usual, He did in His timing and in unexpected ways. I wondered if Dad could someday live with Mom again but never thought it would be possible. Mom was in no condition to care for him.

I had so much to do administratively and financially. We still had the Virginia house to deal with. I had a lot of cleaning to do, the upcoming auction, and hauling remaining personal items to the new home in Pennsylvania. I thought about how much I would love to get back into music again. I'd given up the things I enjoyed because there was simply no time. But God called me to care for my parents. I just prayed that I was up to the task. I was totally dependent upon the Lord for His strength and that is not a bad thing.

Chapter 20: Rehab

For physical training is of some value, but godliness has value for all things, holding promise for both the present life and the life to come.

1 Timothy 4:8

During this time the days were "up and down." I guess I could say that about most days during the storm. Dad had moments where his disposition was good, but he was confused and had difficulty finding words. Mom was obstinate at the rehab facility. She didn't like the hospital bed, stating it was too hard for her back. The rehab center called on the first night and said that we could provide a mattress cover if that would help Mom. Diane and my youngest daughter, who was visiting us, dropped what they were doing to purchase a cover and drive it out to the facility.

It was after 8 p.m. and required a twenty-five-minute drive through wooded areas, in the dark. Anything to make Mom happy. The cover did little to satisfy her.

One evening Mom refused to take her meds and I received a call from the staff. After some discussion and cajoling she finally agreed to take them. From this point until the day she was released, Mom had periods where she could be nice enough to the staff, but she could also be nasty and unreasonable at times. She would text and call incessantly, every day, complaining, and crying to get out. She insisted that she was healed and fine and should be sent home. "How could you put me here? I don't belong here. This place just wants to keep me here to make money," she would protest. As was the case with Dad and his demeanor in rehab, Mom did not do well in a "facility." I knew that God was in this, and we were doing the right thing, but the words still hurt.

Thank God for the staff at the rehab facility. They continually spoke encouragement and reminded me not to take things personally. Whenever I met with the staff, who were gracious, professional, and compassionate, they told me that Mom was progressing, but in no condition to go home, nor live alone. I wondered what that meant for the future. In addition to her physical issues the center noted her cognitive ones as well. I was really discouraged and depressed that Mom was so unhappy, but at least she wasn't bedridden and screaming like she was in Virginia.

One morning the staff met with Diane and me, reminding us that we needed to do some self-care, or we'd burn out. They assured me that they were taking good care of Mom, and we shouldn't feel guilty about not visiting every day. When I say "staff," I am referring to leaders from every applicable department, e.g., nursing, social work, even nutrition. They took their jobs very seriously and gave us their undivided attention. I was impressed and grateful for the care and compassion they exhibited to Mom and us!

At the staff's insistence, Diane and I took a short drive out of town, went to an inspiring movie and shopped. The good people at the rehab facility said that we needed a day to ourselves. I turned my phone off but later saw that Mom had texted and repeatedly called the entire day. When I finally responded to her, she indicated that she was being released the following Friday. I was incredulous because the staff told me that I would first be informed and that a detailed care plan would be in place. I prayed that Mom's statement was not true. How would we care for her? Her house was not move-in ready; Diane was working almost 24/7 to fix it up. I believed that Mom's mind was going, in addition to her physical issues. I was at wit's end, dizzy and nauseated. Fortunately, her statement turned out not to be true.

On March 9th, I picked Dad up from memory care and took him to see Mom at the rehab facility. She was positive, up and about, and looking good. Dad did well, too. I gave them some alone time which was nice for them.

I know that Dad wanted to get out of memory care. I had spoiled him with the visits to the house. He hated going back to the facility. I was in a difficult spot; I understood how he felt and would love for him to live at the house. I just didn't see how it was possible given his behavior last year and present condition. I needed wisdom from the Lord.

On March 12th, Diane and I were in the Philadelphia area for my youngest daughter's wedding shower. I was hoping to enjoy one day away where I could focus on something besides "the storm." Mom texted me throughout the day, indicating that she was ready to leave rehab. I tried to reassure her that the rehab was helping and actually saved her life. My words did little to appease her. The situation was negatively affecting my perspective and walk with the Lord. I felt like I'd lost my sense of love and compassion. I asked the Lord to restore me.

One character flaw I've had since childhood is this: I tend to be my own worst enemy, replaying conversations in my mind, doubting and second-guessing myself, and secretly worrying about what others think. Childhood memories, severe teenage acne, low self-esteem, insecurity, past sins and other baggage still come back to haunt me at times. The second part of 2 Corinthians 10:5 says that "we take captive every thought to make it obedient to Christ." That is something I need to do continually.

I realize that this is all on me and I know that Jesus nailed every one of my sins and flaws to the cross. Thank God that my eternity is secure in Him! Still, I need the Lord's strength and wisdom moment-by-moment to live in His will. Worry is a sin and I must constantly and intentionally go back to Philippians 4:6-8 and other Scriptures to keep my mind focused on "things above." All that matters is what God thinks of me, not man.

When I was younger and would complain to Mom about someone who was picking on me, she would reply with the well-known saying: "Sticks and stones may break my bones, but names will never hurt me." In my opinion, that little proverb is totally false. Unkind words can hurt worse than physical pain. Our words can build people up or tear them down. The Bible tells me so. Proverbs 18:21 says, "The tongue has the power of life and death, and those who love it will eat its fruit." Proverbs 16:24 tells us, "Gracious words are a honeycomb, sweet to the soul and healing to the bones." Harsh words just weigh me down. I am so grateful for those the Lord sent throughout this storm who had words of encouragement for me.

I needed to be reminded that I was once an enemy of Christ, yet He still loves me. I had asked Him to please let me do the same for others. I am not responsible for my mother's happiness. I did not cause these circumstances. The actions I've taken have been to protect my parents, not harm them. And it's what they pleaded with me to do.

A few days after the wedding shower, Mom sounded positive in texts and phone calls. I was and always am grateful for the good moments like this.

To this day, since Mom is living in my town, I feel responsible and sometimes guilty when she is unhappy. I also feel responsible for keeping her occupied with things to do. Most days I am at her house for something, often multiple times per day. And that's okay. In addition to appointments and church, I try to take her out at least once a week for a shopping trip, meal, or event at the senior center.

When Mom complains about her situation to my siblings and others, it's strange but hard to not feel like this storm is somehow my fault. But I take comfort in God's Word. He knows my heart. Psalm 139:1 – 6 reminds me that I answer to my Savior, not any human judge: "You have searched me, Lord, and You know me. You know when I sit and when I rise; You perceive my thoughts from afar. You discern my going out and my lying down; You are familiar with all my ways. Before a word is on my tongue You, Lord, know it completely. You hem me in behind and before, and You lay your hand upon me. Such knowledge is too wonderful for me, too lofty for me to attain."

Mom's release date was finally set for March 20th, officially. I met with the staff on the 16th to discuss her care plan and the way ahead. It was made clear to me that, based on Mom's physical and mental condition, she could not be left alone. I was a little surprised at this assessment, though deep down I assumed she would require some type of help like we had in Virginia.

The reality was, Mom was/is a fall risk with significant memory issues. The facility would be coordinating with an agency to provide 24/7 at-home care for her. We had actually looked into home health care for Mom like we had in Virginia. What we discovered is that it is very expensive, you can only get it for certain hours during the week, and availability is extremely limited. I was impressed and grateful that the rehab center had access to 24/7 in-home care. The fact that they set everything up was a tremendous blessing. I didn't know what the cost would be nor exactly what it would entail, but would soon learn that it was comparable to assisted living. The real benefit was that Mom would be in her own home with some level of independence.

I prayed that things would go smoothly. I was concerned about the cost of memory care for Dad on top of 24/7 care for Mom. On paper we would be okay for a little while, but I wondered about the high cost long-term. Still, what choice did we have? Diane and I could not continue to be full-time caregivers ourselves.

While this was happening, I took Dad to a local eye doctor who performed a long, thorough exam. The hospital in Virginia recommended that we have Dad's eyes examined based on symptoms they observed. The optometrist here diagnosed Dad with "dense cataracts." Consequently, the doctor referred Dad to an ophthalmologist near Harrisburg for possible surgery. I prayed for wisdom; would Dad be able to handle the drive and surgery? We would have to wait almost a month for an appointment with the specialist.

Dad agreed to having cataract surgery and I checked with Mom, my brother and sister to ensure that everyone was in agreement. One thing I've learned is that you need to weigh the risks versus benefits when it comes to surgeries and procedures for elderly parents. It's also wise to obtain family consensus for big decisions like this. Even though I am responsible for making the final decisions with Mom and Dad's health, I never do it in a vacuum. Prayer, and guidance from doctors and siblings are part of the decision-making process. Some tests and procedures, at their age and in their conditions, are not worth it due to the trauma and risks. In this case, based on the doctors' counsel, cataract surgery was considered very safe and could improve Dad's perspective, making it easier to live with dementia.

Diane continued to work feverishly, day and night, on the new house to make it pleasant and nice for Mom. I visited Mom in rehab, took Dad out to lunch and then brought him to my house for a visit. Diane then left for Florida for a pre-wedding trip with the bridal party. My youngest daughter was getting married, and the trip would be a nice break for Diane. I insisted that she have a good time and not worry about anything going on here. She heeded my advice, and we hardly communicated during her trip. That's the way I wanted it, for her sake. She cultivated some new friendships and had a fantastic, memorable time which she still talks about.

Diane and I have been married for over forty years. A young lady in a local coffee shop recently asked me what the secret is for a happy marriage. I don't know about anyone else but, for me, the secret is to put your spouse first (after the Lord, of course). It turns out that this principle is Biblical as reflected in Philippians 2:3-4, "Do nothing out of selfish ambition or vain conceit. Rather, in humility value others above yourselves, not looking to your own interests but each of you to the interests of the others." Serving my wife has been one of life's greatest blessings to me. I find joy in serving and doing things to please her.

As Diane headed to Florida, I made a quick one-day trip to Virginia to continue cleaning the house and to fetch more items. "Quick" meant about twelve consecutive hours between the long drives and time spent at the house. It's a good thing that I made this decision based on the amount of "stuff" I still needed to bring back to Pennsylvania. It would require a couple more trips to get everything moved. On the way I stopped at my favorite coffee shop in Scottsville and got a haircut by a barber I'd gotten to know. I was always blessed by friends I saw on the route to my parents' place in southern Virginia. It was hard to believe everything that was going on; at times it seemed like a bad dream. But I prayed that I was finally coming out of the storm.

Back in Pennsylvania, Dad continued to struggle with words and memory. I visited Mom in rehab and, at first, she was a little negative, but after we talked for a while, she calmed down. I was blessed to pray with a family who's precious ninety-four-year-old grandmother was in her last hours. It was a privilege and blessing to share in this family's grief and offer words of encouragement.

I am grateful for the things God has done in me through this storm. In the past I was uncomfortable visiting nursing homes and assisted living facilities. I avoided them at all costs and had fears about what I would encounter. Being around the memory care facility for Dad and the rehab center for Mom not only gave me an appreciation for the staff, but a heart of compassion for the residents. The residents' smiles and conversations encourage my heart. I thank God for exposing me to this world with which I was unfamiliar. My hope was to become more involved with music ministry in elder care facilities. The Lord began to open up those opportunities for me and I am so thankful and blessed.

Chapter 21: Mom Comes "Home"

But our citizenship is in heaven. And we eagerly await a Savior from there, the Lord Jesus Christ...

Philippians 3:20

I was so grateful to be back in my home church after missing several weeks. I prayed for a smooth transition as Mom was scheduled to come home the following day, March 20th. Mom was walking much better due to her time in rehab. When I brought her "home" to the new house, Mom expressed her displeasure. Diane had done an amazing job, cleaning, decorating and organizing things at the house, but Mom didn't appreciate it, which hurt my wife's feelings. Given Mom's pain, memory issues and all of the changes she was going through, we tried to be understanding and compassionate. Mom did get to visit Dad and take a tour of the memory care facility. She also cheered up a little after dinner. The 24/7 caregiver arrived in the afternoon on the same day.

While it would be an adjustment having someone living in the home with Mom, the caregiver is a Christian woman who grew to love both of my parents. Unfortunately, the house only has two bedrooms, one of which contains "White" (the cat). We had to keep Mom's cats apart since "White" has his claws. Thus, the caregiver was relegated to the sitting room, which contained no bed but a short couch where she would have to sleep. I was concerned that these arrangements would not be suitable, but she never complained, a testament to her character. We have since installed a new bed and privacy screen which she and subsequent caretakers now use and appreciate. It's not a perfect setup, but safe and practical for Mom.

For me, I felt like we were getting part of our life back. Having 24/7 care for Mom gave me peace, knowing that someone was there for her at all times. I would still be responsible for bills, groceries, appointments, medicine, home maintenance, et. al., but at least Mom was mobile and no longer five hours away. I prayed, "Lord, You will bring me through this storm just like You've done for all of Your disciples." 2 Corinthians 4:17 calls these things "light and momentary afflictions."

Diane arrived back home from Florida, and I was glad to see her and grateful that she had a relaxing, enjoyable time.

Mom on the other hand continued to show symptoms of memory loss; she repeated herself constantly. I was feeling overwhelmed with all of the responsibilities. Between Mom and Dad's health problems, managing their finances and bills, maintaining the new house, and still dealing with the old house in Virginia, I wasn't sleeping much. But on a positive note, I was sleeping in my own bed!

The manager of the elder care agency stopped by to evaluate Mom. I was grateful that he is also a strong Christian, so we hit it off immediately. As I've said repeatedly, all throughout this storm God miraculously sent people who were just what I needed, when I needed them. I don't know what we would have done without the great people the Lord sent into our lives. "Darren" wanted to get to know Mom, so he took a walk with her. He spoke sweetly and held onto her so that she wouldn't fall. He listened and allowed Mom to speak her mind. He was very compassionate and encouraging.

Darren told Mom that she was in a good situation and encouraged her to pray. Initially I got the impression that Mom was angry with God because of her circumstances. Deep down I know that Mom has trusted Jesus Christ as her Lord and Savior but the drastic life changes, a move from Virginia to a strange new place, pain and memory issues had clouded her perspective. She grew up with the benefit of two Christian parents and encouraged me in Christian teachings when I was younger. Although I turned my back on God until I was older, the seeds she planted were instrumental in bringing me to faith.

Most Sundays, when Mom feels up to it, we bring her to our Sunday school class and church service. I am grateful that people in my church have compassion for Mom. She is an extrovert and talking with others is good for her, even when the stories are repeated and embellished. I pray that through the Word, the Holy Spirit, worship and fellowship, Mom would realize that God is for her and more than enough for every need. Deep down, I believe that she knows this.

I brought Dad to the house and had him wrapping some quarters he had collected in Virginia. I tried to keep him engaged with activities to give him purpose and keep his mind active. When Darren observed Dad, he (Darren) took me aside and said, "Bob, you need to get your father out of memory care and home with his wife." Truthfully, the comment stopped me in my tracks. I'd never thought that Dad could ever live with Mom again given his condition and all that had transpired. But he was relatively stable, and we had a 24/7 caregiver who could watch him and ensure that he took his medicine. Darren assured me that the agency has expertise in dementia patients and end-of-life care.

I was apprehensive because of Dad's (and Mom's) safety, but was this possible? Memory care saved Dad's life, and the facility was wonderful to him. But he was choosing to spend a lot of time alone there and did not socialize nor participate in group activities. I was told that studies have shown that people do better in their home, with their spouse. I knew that the cost of care would increase but the total would still be less expensive than having both Mom and Dad in an assisted living facility.

Unlike Mom, Dad loved the new house. He never once talked about life in Virginia. He was with family, which is what he had longed for. God was doing an amazing work in Dad's life which made him more mellow and down-to-earth. He lived in the moment and his cooperative and grateful spirit were such a blessing to me. His heart was soft.

It became increasingly difficult to take him back to memory care after spending time at the home. It broke my heart each time I returned him to the facility and escorted him back to his room. Typically, he just sat in a rocking chair, alone. I would bring him snacks and soft drinks he liked, but that did little to make him "happy." Yet, I still wasn't sure if bringing him home was a good idea. Would he be safe and functional? What if it didn't work out and we lost our room in memory care? We'd be on a waiting list again. What was my fallback solution? I prayed for wisdom and recalled God's faithfulness in the past. "Lord, please remove this storm or give me peace of mind in the midst of it ..."

It was the 24th of March, and I headed back to Virginia to clean and pick up more of Mom and Dad's personal "stuff." Mom was mobile again, which was miraculous, but she was unhappy with where she now lived. Mom texted and called my brother and sister continually to lament her situation and plead with them to move her elsewhere. My brother informed me that Mom hated the new home and our town, and wanted to move to New Jersey with my sister. It was discouraging that no mention was made of Dad, his condition, and what he wanted.

I was very discouraged but recognized that something was going on with Mom's mind. Pain and change could only explain so much. I was reminded of Isaiah 26:3 which let me know that my mind needs to be focused on You, not my circumstances. I needed the Holy Spirit to help me. He has never failed me.

Chapter 22: The Auction

Because of the Lord's great love we are not consumed, for His compassions never fail. They are new every morning; great is Your faithfulness. I say to myself, "The Lord is my portion; therefore I will wait for Him."

Lamentations 3:22 – 24

With the chaos in Pennsylvania, I still had my work cut out for me in Virginia. On the way to my parents' place, I stopped by the attorney's office and signed papers required for the sale of the Virginia property. Over the previous weeks I had spent countless hours on the phone and exchanged e-mails with the real estate agent as well as the attorney's office. I thank God for the rapport He gave me with these fine people. Besides their professionalism and expertise, they displayed empathy and compassion for my parents as well as Diane and me. They also got us past several stumbling blocks which could have hindered the sale of the home. But now, things had finally fallen into place to sell my parents' property.

It was Friday and things were all set for the big auction on Saturday. My parents' farm equipment and other items they no longer needed would be sold to the highest bidders. When Diane and I pulled up to the house I was impressed by the setup. Items were tagged, a parking area was established, and a large tent occupied the front yard. Norman, my dad's good friend and helper, met Diane and me as we got out of the car. He joked, "Don't take your shoes off, the auctioneer will put a tag on them for the sale!" It was nice to have a little humor in what would turn out to be a bittersweet weekend.

I am grateful for the real estate agent/auctioneer who originally sold the land to my parents. He would sell off the farm equipment, unneeded furniture, and other odds and ends. He would also donate anything that didn't sell and discard the massive amount of trash. All of that was a big help to Diane and me. Also, by God's provision, the new buyers agreed to adopt the farm animals. The things I had stressed over for years would no longer be a concern. The only thing left for me would be gathering up remaining personal items and performing a deep cleaning once everything was out of the house. All praise to God! That being said, it was still emotional given my parents' lives there and the many memories. This was something I had not anticipated.

The auction on March 25th was something to behold. I've never seen anything like it. The large tent would be where most of the items would be auctioned off. Other items would be sold in specific locations scattered throughout the property. Dad's office, where I remember him most, was turned into the focal point for payment. Although my parents lived in a very rural area, we counted ninety vehicles and over 150 people at the auction. People came out of the woodwork for the sale. There were porta potties and even a food truck! It was quite the event. The organizers did an amazing job parking cars and keeping things moving.

At the beginning of the auction, Rick, the real estate agent/auctioneer paid tribute to my parents. He told the audience that Mom and Dad had established and built the farm and how loved they were in the community. It was heartwarming but bittersweet. I use the word "surreal" a lot because often this "storm" has been like a dream. I wake up sometimes and it doesn't seem real.

As morning turned into afternoon and I saw what was happening around me, the emotions hit, and my eyes swelled up with tears. This is one of the hardest things for me to write in this book. With Mom and Dad's health, I knew that we had done all the right things, not perfectly, but prayerfully, according to their wishes, and with the best intentions. Doctors, lawyers, siblings, trusted friends, even Mom herself: they all encouraged me that we had to do this. But it didn't make it any easier. I wish things hadn't gone the way they did with Mom and Dad's health but here we were. I had been so busy "doing" that I lost sight of the bigger picture and the magnitude of life changes in a short amount of time.

I got emotional thinking of all the memories there and all Dad had done around the house and farm. This was an empty piece of more than twenty acres of land when they purchased it in the 1990s. Dad toiled by the sweat of his brow to design and create most of what was there: the house, barn, garage, lean-tos, pastures, decorations. Mom had a greenhouse, trees and flower gardens scattered around the property. She loved spending time outdoors. So many people came up to me to express their fond memories of Mom and Dad, and their thirty-three years there. Remembering Dad in his office, in his heyday on the farm and in the community, while he was now alone in a Pennsylvania memory care facility, was almost unbearable.

I was standing on the front steps, watching the bustle of activity with the auction, when a couple walked up to me. "Are you Rob?" the gentleman asked. I was a little incredulous and guarded; the only people who call me "Rob" are immediate family or perhaps friends of Mom and Dad's who know of me. I stated, "Most people call me Bob. Are you friends of my parents?" The response shocked me, "No, we are the buyers. We drove up from North Carolina to meet you. We wanted you to know who we are and that we plan to retain the integrity of your parents' farm." You could have knocked me over with a feather and my heart immediately melted! I had not been at the house when prospective buyers came through. I had only heard about this couple who made the offer Mom accepted. And here they were.

I called Diane over and introduced Al and Les to her. I then invited them inside the house for a tour and some history. We hit it off immediately; they are two of the nicest people I have ever met. God could not have sent better buyers to live in my parents' home. I have to interject at this point: as grateful as I am and was for this development, Mom has difficulty accepting the fact that anyone else "lives in her home," regardless of reality. I kind of understand but wish that she could see God's hand in this. The truth is that each of us is a steward of what we have on this earth. When it comes right down to it, we don't truly own anything. One of my neighbors, who has gone to be with Jesus, had a saying: "You never see a U-Haul at a cemetery." Each of us will die (unless the Lord returns before that), and someone else will "own" whatever stuff we have. It's easier said than done but I need to be reminded myself not to hold onto things too tightly.

Mom was incapacitated when she moved from Virginia to Pennsylvania. If by some means she had been able to remain in that home, I don't believe that she would have survived. When she was bedridden, in severe pain, and basically helpless, she acknowledged that fact. She cannot climb steps and access to the house required the use of stairs. Moreover, it was not safe for her to be living alone in a rural, isolated home and the specialized medical care she required was not available in her area. Not to mention how she would ever care for the animals and maintain the property.

As I walked through my parents' almost-empty bedroom, I told my new friends about Mom's health issues and how she had fallen in that very room just weeks before. As we walked into the bathroom, I don't know what set me off, but I burst into tears. Dad and Mom's health, the auction, the impending finality to all that had happened there just hit me like a ton of bricks. Al hugged me and we prayed together. I once again sensed the Lord's hand in all of this. As difficult as everything has been, He was working out a perfect plan, in His perfect timing. God is so good!

Our new friends are farmers themselves and had wonderful plans for the property. We exchanged phone numbers and agreed to keep in touch, which we still do. At the end of the day, when all was said and done, I was sad but grateful.

Chapter 23: The Tearful Goodbye

Those who sow with tears will reap with songs of joy.

Psalm 126:5

O n March 30th I was up at 4 am, preparing to make the final trip to my parents' home in southern Virginia. I would make this trip solo while Diane held down the fort at home. I wasn't certain if my presence was required at settlement, but I still had one more load of stuff to pick up. I also had to finish cleaning so that the house was presentable to the new buyers.

In my quiet time I prayed: "Father please forgive me. I continue to push back on my mother when she complains. There is something wrong with her and I pray for healing. Please help me know how to respond. Thank You for the time with Dad. This is my last trip to Virginia. Please let it go well.

Thank You that everything should be in place for the settlement."

I arrived at my parents' property relatively early. I vacuumed the empty house, did some final cleaning, and loaded my car with the last of my parents' personal stuff. As I walked through the house for the last time, I couldn't hold back the tears. So many thoughts, so many memories, with them and our children. For over thirty-three years my parents lived here. Yes, deep down I resented the fact that they moved so far away and missed so much of our lives. But I still loved them, and we have good memories of frequent visits here. This home made them happy. I know that Mom misses the place. She probably doesn't realize that I miss it, too. But things could not go on this way. My parents' health dictated what needed to happen. This season had to end...

As I made my final walk through the empty home the tears started to flow. The office where Dad spent so much time with his hobbies, where he wrote letters to us. The spa room where the kids slept when we visited. The living room where we all watched "Jeopardy" and "Storage Wars" together. The dining room where we shared so many meals. The porch where we would sit and talk. But Mom and Dad were no longer here. The house was barren and cold. I didn't anticipate feeling this way. It was so final, and a sadness came over me like I'd never felt before.

I walked out the front door, locking it behind me. I took one last stroll around the property, saying goodbye to each horse and donkey. When my parents could no longer care for the animals, I would feed them and give them fresh water on my many trips. I would cut the grass in the pastures while the horses and donkeys watched me. Ultimately Norman took over, but these animals knew me. A farm is not my cup of tea, but I did love these sweet animals.

The two big horses and the one donkey came over to greet me as I walked up to their pastures. I petted them one last time. It was more than I could stand, and the tears flooded my eyes, as they are even as I write this. I was sobbing at this point. My parents had to move. We had no choice. They would die down here if this continued. I knew that and so did they. But that didn't make this any easier. I wasn't expecting these feelings. This was so final.

As I drove down the long driveway towards the four-lane highway which juxtaposed their property, I stopped at the double gate which I had to close before leaving. I shut the gate and then wept uncontrollably. I sat there in my car and called my brother. I could hardly get any words out when he said, "What's wrong?" I said, "I'm leaving Mom and Dad's property for the last time. It's so hard."

After leaving my parents' property, I drove to a hotel in Farmville, about twenty miles away, to spend the night. My plan the next day (Friday) was to visit several businesses in the area and say goodbye to friends I had made down there over the years, people who knew and loved Mom and Dad. Then I planned to hike High Bridge State Park, outside of Farmville, something I've always wanted to do. I was looking forward to a solitary hike and time alone with the Lord, hoping it would give me peace.

Until a few days prior I assumed that I needed to be in town for settlement, but it turned out that only the buyers were required to be present. Early Friday morning I sent a text to Al who was buying my parents' property and wished him and Les well. I asked them to keep in touch. I was blessed but surprised when Al texted back: "Can you hang around, maybe we could go to lunch after we're done with settlement? Les and I have a gift for you and Diane." I hadn't planned to stay but these were now my friends. "Of course, I'll meet you. How is 11:30 at my parents' favorite diner?"

So, I made my way up the gravel road to the parking area for High Bridge State Park. A ranger followed me in and was gracious enough to tell me some fascinating history about the park. I traversed the mile-long bridge, both ways, and then hiked trails that run beneath the bridge. I was alone for most of the peaceful hike. It was just what I needed to reflect on everything and clear my head, as if that were even possible.

I then drove to several businesses, saying my tearful goodbyes to the folks at the local feed store as well as banks my parents patronized. I was blessed by the well-wishes these friends had for Mom and Dad. Al texted me after the settlement, and we met for lunch earlier than planned at the restaurant. I love this couple. It's like we've known each other all our lives.

When lunch was finished, I said goodbye to Sam (my friend and favorite server) and Michelle (the owner of the restaurant). Outside, Al and Les gave me a dozen fresh eggs from their farm (when I got home, I gave the eggs to Mom). They also gave me a hand-carved cross which Al, a skilled woodworker, made for Diane and me. It hangs proudly on the wall in my office, and it is displayed on the back cover of this book.

I headed towards Route 15, the first leg of my five-hour trip home. It was bittersweet. So sad to close the book on Virginia, but a blessing to know that such good people would be living there.

Chapter 24: April "Showers" Bring May Showers

Not only so, but we also glory in our sufferings, because we know that suffering produces perseverance; perseverance, character; and character, hope

Romans 5:3-4

On my birthday in April, I woke up with a wicked headache. It had only been four months since Dad's incident in Virginia. Amazingly, both parents were now living in my town. But Mom was unhappy and there was still so much uncertainty about the future. So much had happened in a short period and God had been working the entire time, but I was feeling overwhelmed. It was affecting my health, and I wasn't sure what to do. I prayed, "Please help me, Lord."

Each time I was with Mom we would have the same conversations. "So and so is ninety years old, still driving and living on her own. Why can't I? How could God do this to me, it's so unfair…"

"Yes Mom, but everyone is different. I had friends who died much younger than I, much too young. This life is not 'fair;' you're the one who taught me that."

Mom always had an answer: "Yeah, but…" And sometimes she'd go in a more personal route, "You have no idea what it's like to be ripped from your home. No one has ever suffered like this. You'd better hope you never have pain like I do."

The conversations got old, fast. Why can't we talk about family and great memories? I'm only trying to do what is best for her. As time has gone by, I've become more patient with the same conversations. She is still my mother and commands my respect. Thankfully, while these conversations still occur, they are not as frequent today. These days it has gotten somewhat better, in large part due to time and the right medications. Moreover, when things turn negative, I can often shift the subject to pleasant memories. Parts of Mom's long-term memory are still relatively good, so we enjoy those conversations.

As time went on, in the month of April, I lined up medical help for Mom and Dad. Mom needed a Primary Care

Physician (PCP) and a dentist to start. We needed to get her medications resupplied and she had a loose bridge in her mouth. The rehab center provided me with a blister pack of Mom's meds and prescriptions to sustain her until she could see a PCP. This was very helpful. To this day I am responsible for managing Mom's meds. Her 24/7 caregiver ensures that she is administered the correct doses at the exact time prescribed. I am grateful that Mom is receiving great medical care. My dentist, who Mom sees now, has done a great job getting her dental health where it needs to be.

At the suggestion of the rehab center and the director of Dad's memory care, I obtained a consultation at a local chiropractor office. Dr. M attends my church and had done his homework; he reviewed Mom's records and knew all about her condition when we had the initial appointment. Although there is no cure, short of major risky surgery, the therapy gives her some relief with managing the pain. She still had bouts of confusion and short-term memory issues but amazingly, she was walking again. These days the pain can run from mild to severe, but thankfully not excruciating as it was in Virginia.

Whenever Mom complained about her circumstances, Dad picked up on that when he visited the house. He so wanted to live in the home but sensed the uncertainty when Mom talked about moving. He reverted to previous behaviors of anxiety, paranoia, and crying. I wasn't sure what to do.

In early April I drove Dad to the ophthalmologist near Harrisburg, Pennsylvania, for tests and decisions regarding possible cataract surgery. Dad had been looking forward to the appointment and wanted to see better. However, when I first arrived at memory care, he was in tears and confused, refusing to go. After some cajoling, I was able to convince him that he needed to see the doctor, so he finally acquiesced.

Dad did really well on the fifty-minute drive. I noticed that he was focused on simple things, and it was heartwarming; "Look at the traffic, look at the pretty mountains." I was starting to understand that Dad's perspective was one of "living in the moment." There was something refreshing about it and I wondered how often I miss the "little things," distracted by worries and concerns which are insignificant. One blessing through Dad's decline has been the time we've spent together and how close we became. While my father ceased to be who he was, he was still my dad and the moments with him were a special gift from God. I got to know him much better than I did when I was younger. And his gratitude was continual; it was my privilege to serve him.

The eye appointment was long and comprehensive. Dad was a little impatient but did well overall. His cataracts were much worse than we thought. The doctor said that the cataracts were so dense that Dad was about five years overdue for the surgery. This spoke volumes to me about the kind of medical care he was getting in Virginia. I don't blame the doctors there; the issue was the distance from specialized care which they really needed.

I was concerned about the surgery because recovery would be long, and swelling would be an issue due to the severity of Dad's cataracts. Still, the doctors informed me that better vision may improve his quality of life.

I was praying that Dad's confusion, paranoia, and depression would improve. I knew that he wanted to be out of memory care and in the home with Mom. I would have loved to accommodate his wishes but was so afraid of the risks. His December incidents in Virginia were still fresh in my memory. I felt guilty whenever I tried to take a break and did not bring Dad to the house. My mind went in circles; I hated that he was alone in memory care. On the other hand, was I doing a disservice by continually bringing him to the house when he may never be able to live there safely? I prayed continually for direction.

On Easter, I brought Mom and Dad to our house for dinner. My oldest daughter and her husband were there as well, which was a blessing to my parents. Dad and Mom were glad to get out and enjoy a home-cooked meal. I had a talk with Mom about finances and the future. There were so many unknowns. Dad wanted to come home and live with Mom. Mom wanted to move.

A few days later I took Diane, Mom, and Dad out to lunch at a local restaurant. Dad really enjoyed the food at this establishment and one of the servers always took good care of us. She was always so sweet to Dad, which he appreciated. When I took Dad back to memory care, he went off the rails. He prattled on about money that was stolen from him. He kept mumbling about $300 or $500 that someone in memory care took from him.

I was incredulous because Dad was not supposed to have any cash in the facility for obvious reasons; anyone could walk in and take the money when the resident wasn't in the room. I also didn't understand where he would have obtained cash to bring into memory care. The facility kept accounts for each resident, and I ensured that Dad had $25 or so there for haircuts or side trips to ice cream parlors the facility would organize. Dad got mad at me when I insisted that I knew nothing about the "lost" stash of cash.

I mentioned Dad's assertions to a staff member who said that they heard the same thing. They humored Dad and told him that the money was "safe." At one point I was told that it was only play money. Someone else told me that the money didn't exist. I never saw cash in Dad's room. I didn't know what the truth was and hoped he would forget about this.

Ever since I've known him, Dad was always accustomed to carrying cash in his pocket. As the dementia worsened, he was obsessive about his money roll, and often misplaced it. Was he hallucinating about the past or was there really money? I was at a loss and felt badly that Dad was mad at me for not believing him. He just would not let it go. I used an old saying to be honest with Dad: "I don't know what I don't know…"

I told the story to Diane who thought that Dad may have taken cash from Mom's handbag when he was at the house. She saw him rooting around in Mom's pocketbook during one of his visits. When I went back to memory care the next day things became clear. One of the staff members told me that the head of memory care tried to talk to me the day before, but I had already left the facility. The staff member said, "Evidently there was some cash. It's in the safe over on the assisted living side, in the office." So, it appears that Dad did take money from Mom and had it in his room. I don't know what he expected to buy with it in memory care, but he always felt safe having cash in his pocket. The staff appropriately and honestly took it from him and secured it.

I made my way to the admin office in assisted living and, sure enough, they were holding several hundred dollars for Dad. I had to sign a paper, stating that I accepted the money. I told Dad that I would secure it at home, in his personal safe. Dad was right after all, and I apologized for not believing him. In my defense, I didn't know the truth so I couldn't get too mad at him. First, he felt secure having cash in his pocket. Moreover, he was pretty slick to abscond undetected with several hundred dollars cash from Mom's handbag!

I wrote this in my journal on the 12th of April:

How much longer can I live this way? Is this what You have called me to do? Every day is consumed with my parents' health, finances, and needs. Feeling guilty that Dad is in memory care. He loves the home, but his dementia is worse. Has some "accidents" before making it to the bathroom. Do I keep 24/7 care? Will Mom accept it? Is the house big enough? Will she want to move away? We have worked so hard. I feel stuck. Please give me wisdom Lord. Please keep Mom and Dad safe, in a relationship with You, with some level of joy. In Jesus's name.

Based on Mom's unpredictable behavior I scheduled a conference call with experts at the elder care agency. The agency representative, who has years of experience with elder care, tried to give Mom perspective on her situation. As usual Mom responded with her "yeah but ..." mantras; "no one has ever experienced pain like I have, I had a great farm and never should have sold it, I don't need 24-hour care, I can live by myself ..." At the behest of the agency, she did agree to take baby steps and perhaps stay the course through the summer. We would bring Dad home on a trial basis, get through his cataract surgeries and Mom's appointments, and reassess in six months. Mom wouldn't live up to this agreement and still made surreptitious plans to move. Thankfully, God's plan prevailed.

In mid-April we attended a baby shower in Baltimore for my oldest daughter. Concurrently, one of my siblings picked Mom up and drove her to New Jersey for a visit. I was grateful that Mom (and we) would get a break. It was also nice that Mom would get to spend precious time with a family member other than me. But this trip caused major issues with Mom's back pain.

Mom was supposed to stay in New Jersey for several days, but we learned that she only stayed for one night. After navigating stairs at my sibling's home, Mom re-injured her back. When Diane and I arrived home from the baby shower, we were surprised to find Mom back at her house, in severe pain. This was déjà vu all over again.

Back when Mom was in rehab, the Occupational Therapist attempted to have Mom navigate a single step. Due to her neuropathy and back issues, she tripped and injured her leg. The therapist made it clear that Mom cannot climb steps. I'm not placing blame, but Mom was not supposed to climb any stairs. She regressed physically to the point where doctors told me that she needed to be in some type of assisted living. Once again, I didn't know what to do except pray.

Each Monday the caregiver agency calls me for a welfare check. On this particular Monday, Mom was in a lot of pain, and I was very frustrated. God, in His wisdom, orchestrated this phone call. The associate who called told me the story of how she cared for her late mother. She had it much harder than I did and encouraged me with her words. She reminded me that Mom has cognitive issues in addition to her back problems. She also said that I was doing all the right things and needed to take charge to protect both Mom and Dad. I sometimes need to make hard decisions for their safety, even if Mom or other family members don't like it. And the thing I'd neglected: I need to pay attention to self-care. I've been doing too much and worrying too much. If I go down, it's not good for anyone.

I prayed, "Lord You are my only source of hope and You are good. May Your Word and Spirit guide me in every aspect of my life."

On April 19ᵗʰ, Dad stayed overnight at the house. We had bought a bed for him to sleep in and I assembled it in the spare bedroom. The stay went well, though Dad was still depressed and confused. His dementia continued to progress, but he was definitely happier in the home than in memory care.

Mom had a chiropractor appointment and the doctor said that she had regressed both physically and mentally. Climbing stairs caused the setback and we weren't sure if Mom would recover from this. The doctor told me that he could only do so much given Mom's present state, and that she may need to go back into full-time rehab. I prayed that we could get Mom back to where she was with her pain. In the midst of the chaos, we celebrated Mom and Dad's 63rd wedding anniversary.

Mom's pain had gotten worse, but I was blessed to secure an appointment with a pain doctor. The doctor read Mom's MRI from Virginia and ordered another X-Ray. Consequently, he scheduled a spinal injection for Mom's L4/L5 vertebrae.

On April 26th, we finally had an appointment with Mom's new family doctor. The first thing we learned is that this doctor was leaving the practice so this would be our first and final visit with her. I was disappointed because she was so thorough and compassionate with Mom. The doctor reinforced everything I and other medical professionals had been telling Mom about her health and living situation. Still, Mom pushed back and went in circles ("but I want my farm, I hate it here, etc."). Even though the doctor told Mom what she needed to hear, Mom didn't accept the doctor's counsel.

After observing Mom's behavior and conducting a memory test, the doctor diagnosed Mom with mild neurocognitive disorder. It was not a surprise based on my experience with her over the past several months. Even the casual observer could see that something is wrong. Mom, however, was not happy with the label and rejected the diagnosis. Regardless, the doctor ordered several tests before prescribing a memory drug for Mom in order to slow the disease. The doctor also referred Mom to a neurologist for further evaluation. Her memory issues are different than Dad's, but still real and evident.

On April 28th, we had a telemedicine call with Dad's psychiatrist who had helped him so much. Mom, Dad, and I went to the memory care facility for the meeting. It was obvious that Dad had regressed, and his decline continued. One of the things Dad would say periodically is, "I'm sorry…" I'd always reply with, "Dad, you have nothing to be sorry for."

The doctor, who I credit with saving Dad's life and giving us extra time with him, observed both Mom and Dad's behavior. He shifted one of Dad's meds an hour earlier to help with sundowning. I was astounded but just shifting the timing of the med helped stabilize Dad. I told the doctor about our plan to move Dad home and hold his memory care room for another month, just in case something went wrong. The doctor agreed with the plan. I am so grateful for the director of the memory care facility who took care of transferring Dad's meds to a local pharmacy.

When the doctor asked Mom a few questions, she exaggerated about life in Virginia, lamented her life here, and repeated herself several times. I quietly mentioned to the doctor that Mom had recently been diagnosed with memory issues. He said, "I can see that…" As we left the meeting the doctor said something encouraging to Dad, and he smiled. Whenever Dad smiled, it made me smile. Smiles were becoming few and far between…

In order for Mom to start on the memory pill she first had to have lab work, an EKG, and a brain scan. Thankfully, the results of the tests were good, and Mom started on the new medicine. I feel like a pharmacist at times. Dad took a number of pills at four different times a day. Fortunately, the pharmacy organized the meds in labelled blister packs which helped me immensely.

Mom takes a number of pills twice a day. I did obtain Mom and Dad's meds from different pharmacies to avoid confusion, but I moved her prescriptions to Dad's pharmacy after he passed to take advantage of the blister packs. I also monitor the meds to ensure that the caregiver administers them accurately and on time.

At this time, Mom and Dad both needed devices to assist with mobility. Dad had to use a walker all the time and he did so willingly. Mom was and is relatively mobile around the house, but she must use a cane when out in public where the terrain is unfamiliar. Doctors have told her that she should be using a rolling walker, but Mom refused due to the stigma. These days she has availed herself of the rolling walker when out in public, and I am grateful for that. It's actually easier on me. Interestingly, she admits that she is comfortable when walking around the house, though she has difficulty getting up from chairs and sitting down. She is still a fall risk. She occasionally also does chair exercises, which are good for her, at the local senior center.

When I take Mom to doctor appointments, I'll often use a transport wheelchair for convenience. It's an ordeal to keep her steady if the distance of the walk is significant. Mom has her pride and wants to be independent, which I understand. Often, she complains when I hold onto her. "I'm fine," is her mantra. But a fall would be disastrous, so I go out of my way to keep her safe. She does not want to end up in skilled care so I do everything I can to fulfill that wish.

While all of this was happening, my youngest daughter was married. We spent a few days in the Philadelphia area for the wedding, which was wonderful. Shortly thereafter, our oldest daughter gave us our first grandchild, a baby boy. Little baby James was born early and isolated in the hospital NICU for several days. Diane and I spent some time in northern Virginia visiting the baby and our daughter. It was nice to get away and focus on other things, though we prayed that our grandson would improve and be released from the hospital. I praise God that he was sent home after several days.

Diane and I stayed in Virginia for a few days while James was in the NICU. On the way to the hotel one night, we stopped at a thrift store where Diane did a little shopping. I browsed for a few moments then sat outside on a bench. A woman, who I came to know as "Alice," asked if she could sit with me. I got to know her and learned that she was from Sierra Leone. She is also a believer. We shared stories and she prayed one of the most powerful prayers I've ever experienced. With everything going on with my grandson and parents, it gave me peace and strength I needed at that moment. Once again, God provided for me through a divine appointment.

We came home and enjoyed a nice Mother's Day dinner at our house. The next morning, I reflected on the trials of the past year and realized how the Lord carried us. There were so many miracles which weren't obvious to me in the heart of the storm. Things started to fall into place as we transitioned Dad from memory care to home. I never thought that Dad could ever live with Mom again. And here they were, in my hometown, together again. All praise to You, Lord.

Chapter 25: Finishing Well

Very truly I tell you, unless a kernel of wheat falls to the ground and dies, it remains only a single seed. But if it dies, it produces many seeds.

John 12:24

Dad made it through both cataract surgeries with flying colors. The procedures improved his vision but not as well as the doctor hoped for. Right after Dad's second surgery, one of the nurses called me back into the recovery room. She informed me that Dad had done very well with the procedure. As he recovered and ate a snack, the nurse said that I could pull the car around to the front of the building and she would bring Dad out. I went outside and parked the car close to the door.

As I helped Dad into my vehicle and closed the door, the nurse placed her hand on my shoulder and spoke these words to me: "I was talking to my colleagues inside, and we think you're doing a great job with your dad." I did all I could to hold back tears as I choked out a "thank you." With everything I was dealing with, with everything that had happened since Dad's incidents at the end of 2022, those words were like healing balm. The pressure, the stress, the second guessing, were all wearing me down. The sweet words from this woman came from God, Himself. I knew that, although it wasn't easy and I made mistakes, I was doing the best I could.

Our words can speak life or despair and, these days, I coveted any encouragement I could get. There are countless books on caregiving but each of us is different and no two situations are the same. In my heart, based on everything that transpired over the past several years, I know that God has held me every step of the way. It has been difficult and is often thankless, but God gives people the right words at the right time to keep me going for one more day.

At the beginning of the summer in 2023, Dad spent most of his time in his favorite living room chair, the one he had in Virginia. He enjoyed watching videos of airport activities, planes taking off and landing. One day, while sitting in his chair, he said to me: "What's wrong with this house? It's everything we need!" My dad's soft heart and positive attitude, in spite of all he had lost, was inspiring.

Dad also enjoyed sitting outside, watching and waving to neighbors as they walked by. While he had lost so much cognitively and physically, we still had some laughs and great conversations. The time we spent together was a precious gift from God. He had to use a walker to get around and enjoyed being with Mom in the new Pennsylvania home. His dementia continued to worsen but, overall, he was relatively stable. However, things would go downhill quickly in late July.

One day when Diane and I were out of town, medics were called to the house when Dad fell and the caregiver could not get him up. Although his vital signs were good and he wasn't transported to the hospital, it became clear that he could not stand well on his own. His dementia was to the point where he had trouble following simple commands such as "stand" or "turn around." He was now pretty much confined to his chair during the day, and to his bed at night.

One night Dad attempted to crawl out of his bed and scraped his lower leg. Due to his circulation and the blood thinners he was taking due to the strokes, his leg had developed an ugly abrasion. I suggested that we go to Urgent Care to have the wound examined and treated, but Dad refused. I cleaned the wound thoroughly and applied triple antibiotic ointment, with the intention of taking him to a doctor if it worsened.

On August 3rd, things took a turn for the worst. Diane and I were in northern Virginia, visiting my oldest daughter and our first grandson. As we were about to leave for home, I received an alert on the security camera I had installed at my parents' home. I noticed an ambulance in their driveway which sent me into a mild panic. It seems like anytime Diane and I take a day off to do anything for ourselves, something happens. I quickly called Mom to ascertain what was going on. Evidently, the caregiver was helping Dad in the bathroom when his legs gave out and he fell to his knees. The caregiver could not get him to his feet. Consequently, Mom called for an ambulance.

Mom told me that the medics got Dad back into his chair. I asked Mom to let me talk to one of them. I learned that Dad's legs were extremely weak and would not support him. Based on that information I asked that Dad be transported to the hospital, and I would get there as soon as I could. We made the two-and-a-half-hour trip back to Pennsylvania, picked up Mom, and headed to the ER. Due to my experience with Virginia hospitals, I just assumed that Dad would be examined and released to return home. As it turned out, the weakness in Dad's legs was just the tip of the iceberg and he was admitted to the hospital. Sadly, but providentially, this was the beginning of the end...

Dad spent five days in the hospital to treat a urinary tract infection (UTI), sepsis, low oxygen level, and several other issues. I was with him every day and often just sat by his side while he slept. All he wanted to do was "get better and come home." At one point I asked him this: "Dad, last year we talked, and you told me that you know Jesus as your personal Savior. You still believe that, right? You know that you're going to heaven?" Dad replied, "Yes." I continued, "I'm proud of you, you've really mellowed out over the past several years." He said, "I had to." While his words were few, I had a feeling of great peace and joy over what Dad had spoken.

Dad would leave the hospital confined to a wheelchair. Doctors recommended that we consider hospice care and I planned to look into that after he would see his primary care physician. The reason I stated previously that the hospital stay was providential is because of their recommendation to investigate hospice. The hospice agency turned out to be amazing and allowed us to keep him comfortable until his passing. I don't know what we would have done without them. In the meantime, the hospital system assigned a nurse to Dad for home visits.

Several days after Dad's hospital stay, he had his first appointment with the primary care physician. Based on Dad's mobility issues I was thankful that his caregiver accompanied me to the office. I could not lift or move Dad by myself, so the caregiver helped me get him in and out of a wheelchair. The doctor was very compassionate, thorough, and understanding with Dad. Based on his condition she also suggested that Dad be referred to hospice, just to get a second set of eyes on him. I agreed and the doctor sent the formal referral to the agency.

The following Saturday, hospice provided a hospital bed which was installed in Dad's bedroom. A nurse from the agency was scheduled to visit Dad on Sunday afternoon to assess his condition. The next morning, I was sitting in Sunday school, preparing to teach the class, when Mom texted me: "Dad fell out of bed and was on the floor. But not to worry; the medics came and got him seated in his living room chair. I just wanted you to be aware…" The hospital bed only had a single sidebar and Dad found a way to slip out. Fortunately, he was not injured. For a moment this made me reflect on last year when I received texts like this from Mom in Virginia. At least I didn't need to make a five-hour trip to deal with the crisis-du-jour. I tried to stay calm.

I went to Mom's house after church and a hospice nurse showed up a little after 1:00 p.m. She spent several hours with us and performed a thorough assessment on Dad. Based on his condition and the likelihood that he was approaching end-of-life, he was formally approved for hospice care as of August 13th. A second sidebar was installed on the hospital bed to preclude another fall.

I cannot over-emphasize that every person associated with the hospice agency, from the doctor and nurses, to the social worker and aides, were professional, compassionate and helpful. They not only tended to Dad's medical needs but also provided comfort and support for Mom and the family. Initially a hospice nurse would visit every three days. Over the next several weeks the visits would increase to daily due to

Dad's quickly-declining condition. They were always just a phone call away and my lifeline in Dad's final weeks.

The following Friday night of that week Mom called and said, "You'd better come over, I think that Dad is dying." Diane and I rushed to the house and found Dad slumped over in his living room chair. He was unresponsive at first, but then spoke repeating, "I'll be okay, I'll be okay..." I called hospice and spoke to the nurse who was busy with another patient and unable to come over right away. She recommended that we get Dad sitting up in the chair, which we struggled to do but finally accomplished. He was able to squeeze Diane's hand, which was a good thing. Dad fell asleep in the chair while we waited for the nurse. As I looked at him, I remembered the strong, brilliant man who accomplished so much and touched so many lives. Dad kept to himself over the years, but we became so close in recent months. Despite his condition, the Lord once again gave me a peace beyond all human understanding. Dad knows Jesus Christ and knew where he was going. He told me so. The Bible says in Romans 10:9, "If you declare with your mouth, 'Jesus is Lord,' and believe in your heart that God raised him from the dead, you will be saved." I trust in God's Word.

The nurse arrived close to 10:00 p.m. We don't know if Dad had a mini-stroke or other medical event but he could not stand or walk. He had no strength in his legs and little in his arms. The nurse recommended that Dad be confined to the hospital bed for his safety and comfort. He would spend the final days of his life there.

As the days went by, Dad was very confused but there were times when we communicated and laughed together. However, his words were very limited, and he was sleeping most of the time. The blessing and answer to prayer is that he was not suffering or in any serious pain. Mom will sometimes paint a dark reality of Dad's final days, but I experienced just the opposite. It could have been so much worse.

The main goal going forward, based on guidance from the hospice agency, was to keep Dad as comfortable as possible. When the nurse was ready to leave, I asked her an honest question: "How long do you think Dad has?" The nurse graciously and compassionately said, "It's up to God of course but, medically, I'd guess two-to-six weeks." It suddenly hit me that Dad, my hero, was on his deathbed.

Here is the thing about Dad: He has always been resilient and would not leave this earth until the Lord was ready to take him home. We knew that this time was coming. For me, it was difficult, and I'd really been mourning Dad for the past several years. Yet I took great comfort in the fact that He knew Jesus as His Savior. Interestingly, Dad would live just over six more weeks, slightly beyond the window the nurse had predicted.

Once Dad was on hospice, the agency was totally in charge of his care. If Dad had any issues, we would not call 911 but rather the hospice number. They took care of everything, which included the ordering of his prescriptions and even grooming. When the time came for Dad to leave this earth, the procedure was to call hospice instead of an ambulance. The agency would coordinate everything for us.

As difficult as this time was, there were many blessings sprinkled in. God has done that throughout this "storm." Mom spent a great deal of time with Dad, holding his hand and speaking to him, even at times when he was not very verbal. Mom temporarily became more focused on Dad than her own issues which was a blessing to me. I took solace in the fact that this is what Dad envisioned when he was in the Virginia hospital. All he wanted was "to be with his family" and he got his wish.

The next few weeks were bittersweet as I watched my father, who lived on this earth for 84 years, deteriorate rapidly. I still spent precious time and had meaningful conversations with him. There was no television set in his room, so I set the computer up to play comforting piano-based instrumental hymns. I will never forget the feeling I had when I walked into Dad's room and heard the sweet, soft music in the background. Medical experts tell me that hearing is the last sense to disappear, so I believe that the music and our words blessed and comforted Dad in his final days.

I loved watching Mom hold Dad's hand and talk to him. One afternoon I brought my guitar over and played familiar songs to which Dad would hum along. When I started to play and sing, "God Bless the USA," Dad said, "I'm going to cry." He loved that song.

I am grateful for the times when Dad was lucid and we could converse. We reminisced about the great times we had in the past. One day I asked Dad, "What is the thing you are most proud of in terms of accomplishments? Military service, career?" Dad's mind was churning but he could not give me an answer. Just to fill the silence I asked, "Do you think I turned out okay?" What Dad said next brought me tears: "You've got to be kidding me..." I am not worthy of Dad's esteem but grateful that he was proud of his son. I know that he was proud of each of his children and grandchildren.

On August 24th, representatives from hospice presented Dad with a certificate, quilt, and flag pin for his military service. I was not present, but Mom told me that it was a touching ceremony. One morning, lying in his hospital bed, Dad asked for the pin. He just wanted to hold it in his hand. It was a great blessing that my brother, sister, and my children came to visit Dad to say their "goodbyes." While that was difficult for them, it was healing because the visits lifted Dad's spirits.

By August 27th, Dad began to get agitated and was crying frequently. Whenever Dad was uncomfortable or his behavior changed, I would call hospice for direction. No matter when I called, 24/7, they always provided the guidance and words I needed. At this point they counselled me to start Dad on a nightly regimen of "comfort" meds to keep him calm and help him sleep. I was under the impression that hospice personnel would administer this type of medicine but that is not how it works. I was told that the caregiver could administer the meds (I'm not sure the agency would allow that) but I felt like I needed to take the responsibility. I believe that Dad was more comfortable with that. It was my honor and privilege to take care of him this way.

Hospice nurses provided me with a supply of comfort meds, measured in the prescribed doses. I kept the medicine under lock and key. I also maintained a detailed record of doses I administered in a diary provided by the hospice agency. Whenever the nurse came over to check on Dad I reviewed the diary with them. As time progressed, I would be administering medicine more frequently so I could not stray far from home.

Dad had collected a host of twenty-five-cent state quarters and had them organized in plastic cylinders, by state. A few months before, he expressed the desire to downsize and deposit the coins into his bank account. The local bank required that the quarters be wrapped into $10 rolls. Periodically I would sit with Dad, and we would wrap coins together. Dad had some difficulty so I would count out the coins and get him started on the wrapping process. He enjoyed performing the simple task with me and it was a special time just being together.

On September 8th, I sat with Dad and asked if he would help me wrap some coins. He was unable to do much in his hospital bed, so I wrapped them and allowed him to close the ends of the rolls. It was a simple task, but I believe that he enjoyed it and found purpose in it. I was thankful to just be spending time with Dad and grateful that he wasn't in any pain save an occasional headache.

I wanted to visit my youngest daughter near Philadelphia, so I asked Dad if he would be okay if I were away the following day. Dad stated to me, as clearly as he could, "Be safe, I want you to live your life." Dad's selfless attitude was contagious. These moments kept me going. God, I miss being able to talk with him.

I felt badly that Dad was confined to a hospital bed, but hospice medical professionals made that decision when he could no longer sit up in a chair. His physical strength was declining rapidly and even slight movements caused Dad extreme pain. There were no other practical options.

From this point on, I did not sleep well. Dad would experience sporadic head and back pain, necessitating administration of increased doses of comfort medicine at all hours. The caregiver would periodically reposition Dad to prevent bedsores. Although Dad was not extremely vocal, we had a special moment where I said, "Dad, I love you." He replied softly, "I love you, too."

On the 10th of September, hospice called me at 2:45 a.m. after they received a call from Dad's caregiver at the house. Evidently, he was awake all night and very anxious. The hospice nurse recommended that I give Dad a dose of medicine to calm him and facilitate sleep. I remember my anxiety as I quickly got dressed and got into my car to head to my parents' house. Yet, on the way, I felt God's peace come over me and sensed a special strength to deal with the circumstances. I wasn't operating on much sleep, but God impressed upon my heart that I was serving my earthly father as he was getting closer to going "home." The strength came from my Heavenly Father. I prayed, thanking God for the time He had given me with Dad, and the supernatural strength and peace He provided.

By September 11th I was giving Dad comfort meds every eight hours based on hospice direction. At this point he was talking about dying and his speech was very difficult to comprehend. The words of Psalm 37:7 gave me comfort: "Be still before the LORD and wait patiently for Him…"

Since Dad was sleeping most of the time, I found it difficult to wake him to administer his medicine, especially in the middle of the night. It would get to the point where I would give the meds as he slept. Hospice nurses advised me that it was better to not wake Dad up for meds when he was sleeping. When I would gently insert the syringes into his mouth he would respond and swallow the meds. I had a strong sense that Dad trusted me to keep him comfortable, although he couldn't express it. These moments were difficult for me but very personal. I will never forget them.

Dad had been under hospice care for a month as of September 13th. On the 15th, my daughters and grandson came to visit, in essence, to say their "goodbyes" to their "Poppy." The visit was a blessing; Dad's spirits were lifted and he even laughed and smiled. The joy was short-lived as Dad experienced severe head pain. I called hospice who had me increase Dad's meds. Dad was sleeping a lot and not eating. Diane actually fed Dad the last food he would ever consume: strawberries. When Dad began to experience pain, Diane reassured him that I was going to give him a dose of comfort meds. He said, "Oh boy," which were the last words he ever spoke. Hospice then discontinued all of Dad's regular medicine as the inevitable was getting closer. At this point the meds would just be a choking hazard. For me, I was emotional and exhausted.

On September 16th things continued to decline. I called hospice because Dad was moaning in pain. I was advised to increase the dosage of his comfort meds. The meds really helped to keep Dad comfortable. The supervisor also spoke encouraging words to me which really helped. When the nurse came and examined Dad, she predicted that he had less than a week. Again, Dad is a fighter and would survive a little longer than that…

The final week of Dad's life is difficult to describe. At times he became restless and experienced moderate pain, especially when repositioned in bed, but most times he was at peace. By the 18th of September the hospice doctor had increased the frequency of his comfort meds to four times a day. He was no longer eating, was losing weight, and slept most of the time. I prayed for a peaceful ending. I praise God for the strength He gave me to endure what I experienced and to witness that Dad did not suffer.

When nurses predicted that Dad had about forty-eight hours to live, I spent some time alone with him, just talking to him and praying. I believe that he heard every word although he could not respond. Then the reality hit me: the hero and strong man I knew was in his final hours. This is when I cried the most tears—uncontrollably and alone. At one point the caregiver, who did an amazing job caring for Dad, came into the room to check on me. She put her hand on my shoulder and quietly comforted me as I wept. Then she left me alone again to mourn which was what I needed to do…

A word about the caregiver who was there for Dad and Mom: She went above and beyond what she was responsible for. She would turn Dad periodically to prevent bedsores and ensure that he was clean. Hospice nurses lauded the caregiver for how she cared for Dad. One nurse remarked, "Amazingly he doesn't have a mark on him!"

I thought about Isaiah 26:3-4 which comforts me when I think I can't take any more: "You will keep in perfect peace those whose minds are steadfast, because they trust in you. Trust in the LORD forever, for the LORD, the LORD himself, is the Rock eternal." Psalm 46 also came to mind and reminded me that God is my refuge and strength, a very present help in trouble. I needed to be still and know He is God. He never let go of me throughout this storm, or ever...

By the 22ⁿᵈ of September Dad's breathing had become very shallow, sporadic, and labored. I went to the house at 5:35 a.m. to administer comfort meds and Mom was up with severe back pain. I thought, "It will be hard enough when Dad dies, what are we going to do with Mom?" Between her pain, memory issues, appointments, and all the administrative things facing me, I was overwhelmed. Mom was vulnerable and I needed to protect her, even though she believed she could live and manage alone. But once again I was reminded in God's Word that He is my hope and would one day make everything new (Revelation 21:5). He has always been faithful and will see me through the storm.

At this point I was giving comfort meds to Dad every four hours. I was exhausted and sad watching Dad decline before my eyes. Yet I was grateful to have him for so long in my life. A little after 3:00 a.m. on the 25ᵗʰ, the caregiver called and told me that Dad had stopped breathing. I rushed over but found that he was experiencing apnea where he would stop breathing for almost a minute and then take a few breaths. Nurses were astounded that Dad was still alive. I knew that the end was near when Dad developed terminal respiratory secretions, also known as the "death rattle."

I spent all day at the house on the 25th, from 3:00 a.m. until 10:00 p.m. Nurses did not believe that Dad would live through the morning, but he did. At 10:00 p.m., since Dad was still breathing, I went home to get some sleep, but I didn't get much. I fully expected that something was going to happen soon. Dad was so resilient, but his body was shutting down.

At 4:04 a.m. on September 26th, 2023, after a long, courageous battle with vascular dementia, Dad passed peacefully into the arms of his Savior. His caregiver called to give me the news. I had lost my hero. In some ways it was a relief because he had not been himself for some time. And I've said all along that I have no regrets because I spent so much time with him. But there is a hole in my heart that I can't describe. It's still difficult now that he is gone.

I notified hospice and headed to the house to confirm that Dad had passed. The nurse, who was professional as well as compassionate, arrived at the house shortly thereafter. He cleaned Dad up so that Mom and I could see him in a more presentable state. Subsequently, representatives from the funeral home came and removed Dad's body. The men were compassionate and sympathetic, another gift from God. In a moment of serendipity, I knew one of the gentlemen; we had worked and played softball together in New Jersey over thirty years ago.

We had an appointment at 10:00 a.m. to make arrangements at the funeral home. My brother drove from New Jersey to be with us. He, Mom, the caregiver, Diane and I went to the funeral home. Since Dad would be cremated, the funeral home gave us an opportunity to say our last "goodbyes." They set Dad up in a private room so that we could pay our final respects. I wasn't expecting this, and can't explain it, but there was something healing and beautiful about having those final moments with Dad.

Recently I was going through some of Dad's files and came across an undated birthday card sent from his mother (Grandmom Jones). The words gave me another glimpse into the person Dad truly was. The outside of the card has the word "Son" in big letters. On the border are the words "Honesty, Strength, and Integrity." Bookended by Grandmom's words, "Dear Bob" and "Love to you always Mom" are the printed words in the card: "The values you live by make you someone very special, someone to be proud of—Son, you're loved more that you know. Happy Birthday." On the left side of the card Grandmom wrote this to Dad: "I will never forget the things you did for me when you were a little guy. Always thinking of me." A generous heart was characteristic of who Dad was. And I'm thankful for his example which I try to model.

At the end of the personal story he wrote for me in 2016, "Reflections on my Journey of Life," Dad said this as a final thought on the last page: "I've had a stroke and at my current age of 76, creeping rapidly to 77 years old, I thank God each morning that I'm able to awake."

Life is indeed a precious gift from God. Thank you, Dad, for teaching me to be grateful.

You finished well, Sir. I'm so proud of you.

Chapter 26: This is Not Goodbye

For now we see in a mirror, dimly, but then face to face. Now I know in part, but then I shall know just as I also am known.

1 Corinthians 13:12

There was a short period of time where I was numb and wondered what I was going to do. There were so many tasks to accomplish now that Dad was gone. Reflecting on his final days, there is so much for which I am grateful. It was truly a precious gift from God and a miracle, in my mind, that Dad was able to come "home" and live out his final months with Mom. From the time he was admitted to the hospital in Virginia, all he desired was to be with Mom and close to his family. There were so many hurdles and moving pieces, but it all came together. I am thankful that his wish was fulfilled. Above all, Dad made a confession to receive Jesus Christ as his Savior. He finished his race well. We know where he is, and all glory goes to God! That is the best part of his story!

I cannot say enough about the hospice agency and the funeral home which took care of Dad's arrangements. Both entities handled many of the administrative details which made life easier for me during a difficult time. They provided wisdom and guidance for things that I did not know, nor had thought of. As stated before, Dad's caregiver also went above and beyond her call of duty to care for Dad and his needs before he passed. I would have been lost without her expertise and help.

We had planned two services for Dad: the first in South Jersey where Dad spent most of his life. The second would be held in southern Virginia where my parents spent their later years. Like many other circumstances in this storm, there were some bumps in the road. But as usual, God provided exceedingly, abundantly, more than I could have asked for or imagined.

I had planned the first service for October 9th in South Jersey. Most of our remaining family is in that area, including a number of friends. Based on my parents' wishes, Dad was cremated, and we purchased "niches" in the cemetery where my maternal grandparents are interred. Originally, we planned to have a simple service at a "chapel" on the cemetery grounds and this was stated in the obituary. Dad did not care for a lot of fanfare. However, it turned out that the "chapel" was really a covered mausoleum with no electricity or facilities. After talking to Mom and praying about it, I attempted to quickly find a church in South Jersey which would accommodate us.

We were crunched for time, and I called several churches but never spoke to a human being; I could only leave phone messages. None of my calls were immediately returned which was disheartening, but God had a better plan. A few days later I received a call back from a church in the town where I grew up. I had never been to this church, but the pastor was friendly, compassionate, and totally accommodating. We hit it off immediately and miraculously, he offered to host the service on October 9th. The funeral home amazingly and graciously changed the obituary, and we got the word out, to the extent we could, that the venue had been changed.

The service in New Jersey was beautiful; simple and exactly what Dad would have wanted. The added blessing is that the venue was in the town where I grew up and Dad worked for so many years! Pastor Bill, who is now a close friend, facilitated everything and even recorded the service for us. We reconnected with family and friends, including my best childhood friend who I had not seen in about forty years. Fortunately, only one person showed up at the cemetery based on the original obituary. Thankfully, he did make it to the church in time for the service!

I am so thankful that Mom was able to make the three-hour trip to south Jersey, though it was challenging with her pain and physical limitations. I asked Pastor Bill to give the closing prayer at Dad's service. He began by saying: "I did not have the privilege of knowing Mr. Jones, but one thing I do know, is that a man is known by the legacy he leaves. And he's left a wonderful legacy." What a fitting tribute to my father!

We held a subsequent service in southern Virginia on November 4th. Again, through God's orchestration, we secured the church of a friend with whom I attended a service earlier in 2023 during the height of the "storm." I contacted several people in southern Virginia who knew my parents, to get the word out. Mom and Dad spent over thirty years there and made lots of friends and relationships.

Mom was not able to attend due to her back issues and the long drive. This was a very informal service and a tremendous blessing to reconnect with a number of friends who came to honor Dad. I opened up the floor to testimonies and was blessed by the memories people shared, a number of which I had never heard before. The stories were consistent about Dad's kindness, generosity, and sense of humor. He left a legacy in southern Virginia as he did in New Jersey.

Diane and I travelled to Virginia the day prior to the service to tie up some loose administrative ends for Dad. We visited "Baines," our favorite stop, along the way where we enjoyed great coffee and fellowship. After dropping off a donation for Mom at a local charity, Diane and I walked to the barber shop where both of my parents received regular haircuts. The manager, Linda, was not aware of Dad's passing. We spent almost an hour with her, reminiscing about Mom and Dad.

Linda shared a story that I was not aware of, and it brought me to tears. She told us that her business, like many others, was shut down in 2020 due to the pandemic. A few days after she reopened, Dad showed up for a haircut. After he paid the bill, he handed Linda $100 and said, "This is for all of the haircuts I missed during Covid." She never forgot about Dad's kind gesture. That story says it all about Dad's generous heart. That is who he was. I pray that I can model his Biblical qualities, namely his generosity and love for people, for my remaining years.

Chapter 27: Blessings and Trials

Praise be to the God and Father of our Lord Jesus Christ! In His great mercy He has given us new birth into a living hope through the resurrection of Jesus Christ from the dead

1 Peter 1:3

If it were just Dad the story would end here. But the fact is, this story is still being written and the storm simmers. It may go on for months, perhaps years. I could leave this book open-ended and wait to finish it, but I don't know what the future holds. So, after much prayer and feedback from trusted friends, I'll wrap it up with a few things I've taken away from the past number of years. Based on history and experience, I know that my Lord and Savior Jesus Christ will continue to teach and guide me until the day I leave this earth.

First, I've learned that no matter who we are, we can't escape the storms. They are a part of life in this fallen world. The wonderful truth is that in Jesus we have peace because He has overcome this world. In fact, in John 18:36 Jesus said, "My kingdom is not of this world...But now My kingdom is from another place." This storm has not been easy, and although I sometimes get anxious, I don't need to fear the future. His kingdom is from another place, much better than what we see in this broken world. If you're a follower of Jesus Christ, redeemed by His blood, you belong to a different kingdom. While we physically exist on this earth, our citizenship is in heaven. That truth brings me great comfort and joy.

The second thing I've been reminded of is that God absolutely loves me and hears my prayers. That truth has become more real to me than ever. He may not answer according to my will or desired timing, but He is good and has been with me throughout this storm. Romans 8:28 states: "And we know that in all things God works for the good of those who love him, who have been called according to His purpose." Isaiah 55:9 tells us, "As the heavens are higher than the earth, so are My ways higher than your ways and My thoughts than your thoughts." Even when I can't see past the storm, when I don't understand why, He loves me, He is good, and I need to trust Him.

The third thing I've learned is that our words matter. Too often I've turned James 1:19 on its head and have been slow to listen, quick to speak, and quick to become angry. I pray that through this experience that I have become more apt to listen, slow to speak, and slow to get angry. The people God has sent my way, with the right words, has helped to carry me through this storm, and I praise Him for that. I think of Proverbs 16:24: "Gracious words are a honeycomb, sweet to the soul and healing to the bones." It also reminds me to be an encouragement to those I encounter. Everyone is going through something.

If there is one word which characterizes the past several years it is "unpredictable." Some days it seems like nothing goes right. Other days things are okay. I think that it's easy to have "faith" when things are going smoothly, when life seems great. But true faith is exposed when you go through a serious trial. I pray that I've learned and continue to learn that my only hope is in Jesus Christ.

I'm not sure what "normal" is anymore but that's fine. Now that Dad is gone, I'm still adjusting and processing it all. On the one hand, I'm doing okay because I got to spend so much precious time with him. I have no regrets about the way Dad finished his race. On the other hand, I'll sometimes break down into tears because reality just "hits me." Even though for the past several years he was not the man I knew, he was still "Dad," and he was still here. I can't see or talk to him any longer, at least on this side of heaven. But God did a work in him and he was grateful until the end. And he of all people would want me to live my life. We are still adjusting and trying to get some of our lives back. That's what Dad would want.

Most significantly, we had the gift of several extra months together. While it wasn't perfect, Dad got to die at home, with his wife by his side, not in a hospital or a facility. That is how he wanted it, and I am so thankful that the Lord made it all happen. Please don't miss that statement: God made it happen, not me. Again, He was working out all things for my good, for His glory.

If it were just Dad, this storm would be over. But now it's just Mom. We have our good days and bad days. As far as her physical issues, periodic epidural injections, medicines, chiropractic treatment, and physical therapy have helped to keep the pain at bay. But over time the injections have become less effective. Recently she had the successful implant of a spinal stimulator which has helped to alleviate her pain. The device does not resolve her back issues but provides a less-invasive solution. While she is still a fall risk with limited mobility, I praise God that she can walk and has some level of independence. When she left Virginia, she was totally immobile.

As far as Mom's cognitive issues, long-term memory is intact for the most part but it's patchy; she can vividly recall certain things from the past but often conflates timelines and events. Her short-term memory, on the other hand, manifests itself in confusion, repeating statements multiple times, and forgetting conversations and events that just occurred. Medications help to arrest the progression of the condition, but her memory is not getting any better.

There are times when Mom is depressed and has meltdowns, especially later in the day. Some days I handle things better than others and continually need God's grace to be more sympathetic and understanding. Mom has lost a great deal, and I can't imagine the pain she experiences, physically and mentally. She is the only Mom I get and I am thankful to still have her, so we carry on.

When Mom is in pain, all of the focus is on getting her relief. When the pain is relieved, Mom often laments that she could live alone and once again go back to the life she had in Virginia. I am not an expert on cognitive issues but understand from her doctors and books I've read that some things in her mind will not be changed; she lives in a new reality. And I need to be more understanding of that and patient with her. Sometimes it's easier said than done.

We are grateful that Mom still has 24/7 in-home care. My wife and I could not live without it and neither can Mom. While it's not a perfect situation, the care allows Mom to live in her home with some level of independence. Mom will periodically state that she doesn't need full-time care. Her conditions indicate otherwise, and medical professionals have confirmed that she needs it. Mom cannot cook for herself, nor can she take care of the home. She also needs to take medications twice per day and needs to be reminded by her caregiver. Mom sometimes needs help getting out of bed and off of the couch. If she would fall or have a pain spell, like she did in Virginia, it would be disastrous, and she would likely be in a facility—or worse.

Speaking of caregivers, the Lord has blessed us with those who have come to stay with Mom. They are not only compassionate, professional, and empathetic, they actually pray with, and provide companionship for Mom. They go above and beyond what they are tasked to do and we so appreciate it. Diane and I have become close with each one and consider them "family." Amazingly they keep in touch with us even after they return to their homes. I know it sounds strange, but this is yet another blessing we wouldn't have experienced if not for this storm.

Diane and I are still with Mom almost every day but have more freedom than we did when Mom was living in Virginia. We are grateful that we have more time and opportunity to visit our three girls and grandchildren. I am able to teach Sunday school again and provide music ministry in church—things I love and am passionate about. Diane is also free to engage in activities she loves to do. We cannot be with Mom 24/7, nor do we possess the skills to provide the level of care she needs. It may sound selfish, but we do not want to go back to the life we had in Virginia when Mom was in excruciating pain without proper medical care. Those were difficult times which seriously affected our health and well-being. I don't want to repeat them.

Mom lives just three miles from us, and I am grateful that we no longer have to make the long commute to Virginia. Still, we cannot venture far from home for too long. My wife and I have to deal with any health or home "emergencies." In a real sense, we are always "on call" and the first line of defense when it comes to caring for Mom.

Back in late 2023, a few weeks after Mom was feeling relief from a bilateral injection, Diane and I drove Mom back to southern Virginia to meet with a good friend there. We met at a restaurant about an hour from her former property. We decided not to drive all the way to Mom's former residence for a couple reasons: First, it would be a longer drive and riskier with her back conditions. Second, I felt that it would be too emotional if Mom saw her old place. The visit was a blessing for both Mom and her good friend.

Diane and I left Mom and her friend at the restaurant for a few hours to allow them to catch up without our interference. When we returned to take Mom home, she and her friend asked if going forward they could meet every three months. I am more than happy to do that for my mother if her health allows it. Thinking about Mom's health and immobility when she left Virginia, I consider it a miracle that we were able to pull off this visit!

When Mom is up to it, we take her shopping, to Sunday school and church, and to the local senior center where she can enjoy chair exercise, Bible studies, and fellowship with others.

On August 18th, 2024 Diane and I were blessed with a second grandchild, Aubree, born to my youngest daughter. When our granddaughter was just a week old, we took Mom to see her, which was also a great blessing. Mom has also had opportunity to spend time with James, son of my oldest daughter. If Mom were still living in Virginia, she likely never would have met her great-grandchildren. For this and a myriad of other things, I am eternally grateful to my Lord.

Another small trial among this all was that sadly, on January 18th of 2024 we did have to say "goodbye" to White cat as well. He had lost a great deal of weight, was not eating, and appeared to be in pain. It was such a hard decision, but we did not want to see him suffer. We were blessed to find a veterinarian who came to Mom's home and compassionately took care of things. White was by Dad's side when he passed. Now White would pass in the same room where Dad did. Yes, he was a cat, but still part of Dad's story. He was also my buddy for the past two years, so the loss hurts.

I am grateful for the periods of time when Mom can be sweet, and we laugh and have meaningful conversations. Lately, in answer to prayer and likely the right medications, I see glimpses of the mother I knew. I am so grateful to God for those moments. Recently I spent a few hours with her watching our Sunday church service online. Mom was really upbeat and said to me, "You know, I'm no longer afraid to die." I wasn't sure where that came from but probed a little further. "Mom, I've never heard you say that. You have a Christian heritage and asked Jesus to be your Savior years ago. Do you still believe that and know that you'll go to heaven when you die?" Mom said, "Yes, I do." For years I prayed for my parents' salvation and believe, by both confessions, that Dad is there, and Mom will join him one day. This knowledge is the greatest blessing I've received in this storm.

Doctors have told me that my wife and I cannot continue at this pace and are at risk of burning out. I don't take that counsel lightly and have gotten involved with a few support groups from our county's area agency on aging. I am still trying to find an acceptable balance and that will be the case until we face some critical decisions. For now, we are "maintaining" and taking things one day at a time. Caring for Mom's medical needs and finances is relatively easy, and I have those things under control. The most challenging part is protecting Mom from bad actors who try to take advantage of her, through phone calls and texts. It's also a challenge to keep Mom from making unnecessary purchases online. We want her to have independence but there is a fine line between that and having to untangle bad decisions she makes.

While this storm has been full of so much uncertainty, I have a deep inner peace with where things are. I know at some point we may have to take more drastic actions. But for right now, while life is not "perfect," we are giving Mom an independent life while trying to enjoy more freedom for ourselves. If/when the time comes to change things, I am confident that the Lord will direct me and provide the wisdom I need.

God has proved Himself faithful, time and time again. He did so many good things that cannot be humanly explained. I pray that this storm has made me a closer follower of Jesus Christ, imperfect, but cognizant that I need Him moment-by-moment, day-by-day.

Each morning, I begin the day with gratitude. When I wake up, open the curtains, sit and look out at the breaking morning (with a fresh cup of coffee, of course), I thank God for the gift of a new day. Starting the day with a grateful heart gives me perspective that, no matter what is going on in my personal life and in the world, He is good, faithful, and in control. I "count my blessings" as the old song says. In this storm, and at other times in my life, when I hit what seemed like rock bottom, I couldn't see the light at the end of the tunnel. There seemed to be no way out, no happy ending. But God always makes a way, not necessarily according to my wishes or desires, but in His perfect will. I need to trust that He alone has my best interests in mind. Even though I gave Him my life over thirty years ago, this storm has taught me that I was still too self-reliant and dependent upon the wrong things. I still have much to learn and am reminded that I have very little control.

Maybe you're going through a "storm" of your own right now. Perhaps in a circumstance you didn't choose. It may be very painful, and you don't see a way out. I don't know your situation so I can't offer up any platitudes or sugar-coated words. I have no pithy sayings or advice because storms can be difficult—and long. They are also personal and hit all of us differently. It's your storm and only you and God fully understand the magnitude. Please know that my heart goes out to you. As I write this, I'm stopping to pray for anyone who is experiencing a trial or a crisis. All I can do is encourage you with the fact that God is real, His Word is true, and He is for you.

If you have surrendered your life to Jesus Christ and placed your faith in His finished work on the cross for the forgiveness of your sins, you have hope and a secure future. In His way, in His perfect timing, He will deliver You. You may not see it until sometime in the future, or maybe not until Jesus returns, but He is in control and is working everything for the good and His glory. If you haven't surrendered your life to Christ, I pray that you will do that right now. There is no better time and no more important decision you'll ever make.

The key to surviving storms, at least in my experience, is simply staying close to Jesus. Love Him with all of your heart, pray, be in His Word, and trust Him. He is present with you, which is an amazing comfort! When you hit bottom, Jesus is all you have. But He is also all you need, and He is more than enough.

Whatever "normal" was, is gone, and I've accepted that. "That phone call," as I wrote about in my first book, could come at any time, and that reality is always in the back of my mind. But I take solace in the fact that He will give me the strength and wisdom I need to face whatever is to come. He has drawn me closer than ever to Himself over these past several years. And that's more than enough for me.

God is still good, is still on the His throne, and is present with those who love and follow Him. Our home is not in this world but with Jesus Christ. I need to keep my eyes fixed on Him, the One who saved me and gave His life for me. Keep looking up, continue running the race He has established for your life, and don't give up!

Then Jesus told His disciples a parable to show them that they should always pray and not give up.

Luke 18:1

Postlude

The Lord gave and the Lord has taken away;
may the name of the Lord be praised.

Job 1:20b

It is early May of 2025 as I finish the final edits for this book. I've been thinking about the damage this storm has left behind and how God has sustained us.

A few weeks ago, my wife, Diane, spent several days in the Washington, D.C. area to help care for our young grandson. My oldest daughter was recovering from sinus surgery and had limitations on lifting.

Early Thursday morning of that week, while lying alone in my bed, our remaining cat, "Lee Lee" woke me from a sound sleep. She was crying uncharacteristically. It was 2 a.m. and I quickly determined that something was wrong—she was in obvious pain and not "herself." As you recall from earlier in the book, I lost her sister, "Ginger," less than a year ago as she died in my arms.

I called a 24-7 veterinary hospital and ensured that a doctor was available to examine "Lee." The receptionist told me to head down, (about a twenty-five-minute drive), as soon as I could. I was unable to locate our cat carrier, so I picked Lee up and placed her in the back seat of my vehicle. I knew that she was in pain because normally she would fight me if I picked her up. She cried the entire trip, and I was thankful to arrive safely at the hospital, close to 3 a.m.

A visit to the emergency vet is never quick but the staff was compassionate and thorough. Lee is almost seventeen years old and obviously near end-of-life, but I was not ready to let her go. Not like this. After giving Lee a thorough exam, the vet gave me hope as she believed a prescription med could give Lee some extra time. I arrived home at 6:30 a.m., hopeful.

I called Diane and told her what had transpired. I got a few hours of sleep and ran a few errands.

When I arrived home, Lee was very sick and in pain. I called our regular vet and was thankfully able to get an appointment. I knew deep down that she wouldn't be coming home; it was time, and I tearfully had to say goodbye to her. With both cats now gone and Diane in D.C., the house seemed so empty. To say that I was sad and numb would not adequately describe how I felt. I know that so many others have experienced or are going through worse, but it still hurt. This just added to the memories of the long goodbye with Dad, Mom's ongoing health issues, and losing Ginger, as well as "White Cat."

The next day, Friday, I was scheduled to drive to Washington to pick Diane up in the afternoon. I needed some solitude, some alone time with my God. I planned to stop at a state park along the route to Diane. I had passed this park several times and always wanted to check it out. My heart was heavy, and I just desired a solitary hike.

When I arrived at the park, I asked a visitor if I would need hiking poles. He indicated that the trails can be steep and that poles were necessary. So, I grabbed my poles and headed toward one of the trails, reflected in the picture at the beginning of this chapter. I had no map, no knowledge of these trails, nor any cell phone reception. I had no clue where I was going. Looking down the unknown trail reminded me a lot of the past several years: In a sense, when it came to caring for Mom and Dad, I had headed down a path, with unknown difficulties, to an unknown destination.

The first part of the hike was relatively easy. The ground was flat, it was peaceful, and I was totally alone in the woods. It was just what I needed this day. Then the trail I was on became drastically steep. There were times when I thought about turning back because I didn't know where the path would take me. "What if I roll an ankle or get lost? Would anyone find me?" I wondered. After several steep climbs my legs began to hurt. I am in relatively good shape, but I also had to stop a few times to catch my breath. When I started to feel "alone" I was quickly reminded that I had a companion with me—my Lord and Savior, Jesus Christ.

Deep in the woods, when I would encounter another steep incline, not knowing where it went, I prayed, "Lord, please help me find my way." As He always has, God gave me the strength, that "extra gear" to keep going when I thought about turning back. I was reminded that this was also a vivid metaphor for the past several years. God has given me the wisdom, strength, and guidance I needed along the way. And I sensed that He had a blessing waiting for me if I would keep going and not give up.

A short while later, I concluded that I was lost. I didn't know if I was on a real trail nor where the path would take me. After an hour or so I came to a flat area with markings.

The sign literally showed eight different paths. I wasn't sure where to go but needed to make a choice. About fifty feet away, I noticed a group of five headed my way. I asked for their assistance. The group was headed up towards the Appalachian Trail (AT). I did not want to go that far because I needed to pick Diane up in a few hours. They suggested that I turn left a few feet ahead and head towards a summit which would provide a beautiful view of the valley. I thanked the new friends and headed that way. The Lord again brought a parallel metaphor to mind: He sent the right people at the right time to encourage and guide me.

The hike to the summit was challenging. Some signs along the way were confusing, but eventually I came to a clearing with the most beautiful view. The climb was totally worth it. I sat for over thirty minutes, just taking in the scenery, God's beautiful, awesome creation. I soaked in the breeze which reminded me that God's Holy Spirit was with me. I truly worshipped my Lord, thanking Him for the strength He has given me over the past several years. I praised Him for the lessons He has taught me. And I expressed my gratitude for the beauty He brings from ashes. Yes, the storm has brought loss, but also tremendous blessings I otherwise never would have experienced.

The unknown destination of that path I had never travelled was known by God. It was true in that park, and it's been true in this storm. I don't know where I'm headed next in the storm, but I know that He will lead and be present with me. His Word tells me so and I've witnessed it time and time again. To God be the glory!

Mom, Dad, and me. Circa 1961.

Dad's Air Force picture

Dad's favorite picture of him and Mom. He had it framed as a gift for me. It is proudly displayed in my office.

Family portrait of Mom, Dad, my younger sister and brother, and myself. The date is unknown, but it was sometime in the mid-late 1970s.

Dad and I in Texas, 1983

Dad and Mom at our wedding

Dad as postmaster in New Jersey. He was happy to see his oldest granddaughter on a surprise visit!

Dad, Mom, and me. Happier times at their Virginia place.

Dad on the farm, living the dream.

Dad, building a feeding area for the horses.

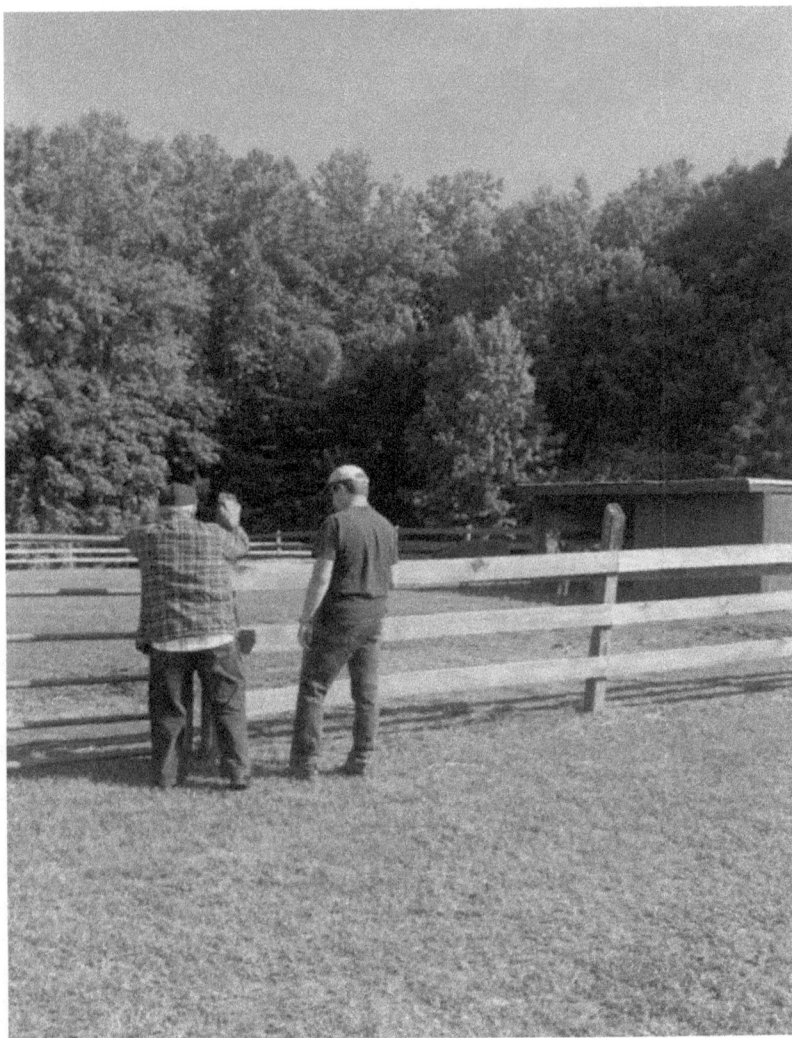

Dad giving me advice on how to repair a pasture fence.

Christmas at their Virginia home. Dad in his favorite chair.

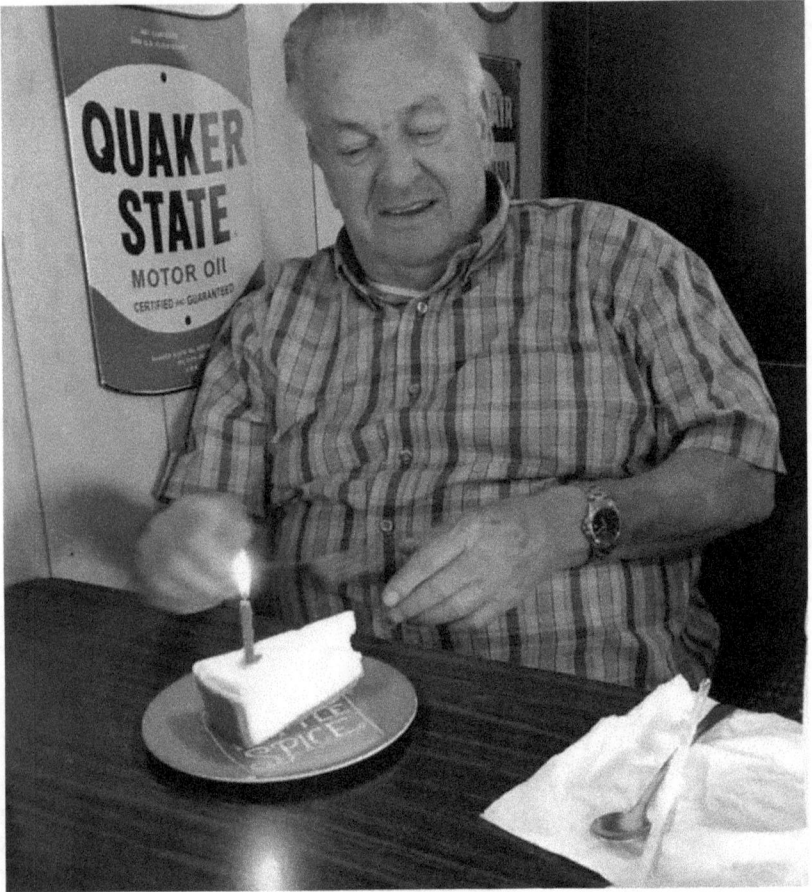

Dad's 80th birthday. We celebrated at his favorite restaurant in Virginia.

In the Pennsylvania house, Dad seeing "White" for the first time in months.

Dad in Pennsylvania, 2023. The smile warms my heart.

"Childhood" by Robert W. Jones

With intricate thoughts possessing his mind,
he passed through the previous years.
To a far distant land, with beauty so grand,
a place for the shedding of fears.

With dew on the ground, the sun in the east,
he saw it was still early morn.
Milk bottles clanged, the town was awake,
a new day was starting to form.

He ran cross a lawn, jumped down off the curb,
then darted out into the street.
His heart filled with joy, his eyes swelled with tears,
at the feeling of youth in his feet.

He slowed down his pace and started to walk,
filling his lungs deep and long.
He walked on a carpet of magical dreams,
Then shattered the air with a song.

A kick at a pebble, a shoo at a bird,
a simple hello to a friend.
All the components of one happy kid,
whose day never comes to an end.

But that isn't true, for this man today,
of youth he has not a trace.
He looks in a mirror, through the stubble of beard,
a thin smile arouses his face.

But now he's content, his dreams have been filled,
of this he is glad, for they should.
Like everyone does, he had just reminisced,
of that wonderful place called "childhood."

Copyright 8/8/2007   TXu1-354-037my

About the Author: Robert Jones

Bob Jones is an average guy originally from New Jersey. He is the author of *Average Man, Almighty Companion* and *Family Love Letters* which are very personal stories. He is passionate about building relationships, encouraging others and sharing the love of Jesus Christ with everyone he meets. He enjoys writing, reading, hiking, worship leading, singing, and playing the guitar. He has been married to his best friend Diane for over forty years, has three grown daughters, and three grandchildren. Bob makes his home in south central Pennsylvania.

You can connect with Bob through his Facebook page at: https://www.facebook.com/RobertJ5999/

Additional copies of this book may
be purchased on Amazon.com

Praise for
IF IT WERE JUST DAD

Have you reached the point in life where you are completely overwhelmed? When you just cry out, "It's too much! If it were just ... ?" You are not alone. I urge you to make the time to take a walk with Bob. His conversational style invites you to come along side as he relates a most personal journey. You will be encouraged. At times it is joyous, and at others, heartbreaking. "The reality is, there are things in life we cannot control, perhaps most things." But there is hope in the midst of the storms of life. His name is Jesus.

Rev. William H. Cook is co-host of the Adventure Pals radio show and Senior Pastor of Creek Road Bible Church in Bellmawr, NJ

If you have ever navigated the minefield of elder care, you should definitely read *If It Were Just Dad*.

Bob, at his story telling best, invites you to ride along on his many trips down I-81 to deal with his latest familial issue. Thanks to Bob being a disciplined journal keeper, he gives you an accurate inside look at how God answered his prayers time and time again, with the Holy Spirit giving him the strength to overcome obstacle after obstacle.

Rick Alexander, Operations Manager Alpha Media (Retired)

In his book, *If it Were Just Dad*, Bob has written a realistic and challenging saga of walking through the issues of dealing with aging parents, most of it while living five hours away from them. He presents the joys and heartaches of caring for them through latter years of their lives as they were dealing with physical issues and dementia. He watched his father change from a strong decisive and creative personality to one who was now dependent on others to care for him in his weakness and loss of mental acuity. He watched his mother try to care for things at home and a small farm for which she was no longer able to perform because of her aging body and mind.

Bob found great help and encouragement through prayer to God and from the many passages of Scripture that he shares at the beginning of each chapter and throughout the book. Bob uses a word near the end of the book that best describes his life with aging and declining parents; the word was "unpredictable." I recommend the book to be read by those dealing with aging parents.

Ron Cook, friend and former pastor

No one wants to think about their parents' final days, but we all have or will experience it. If It Were Just Dad brings us into the personal memories of Bob and his family that help us learn and experience what walking through the last years of his parents' lives were like. This book shows me the power of keeping a detailed journal that brings the power of God to life in our lives. Through this story, we can see real life struggle, doubt, pain, and heartache, and how all those things are answered in the person and work of Jesus Christ. It shows me the impact of personal sacrifice and how quantity and quality time with loved ones will create memories that will truly last a lifetime.

Kevin Greene, Lead pastor of ConnectUs Church

Bob's book is saturated with Scripture! God's Word is always comforting, encouraging, and uplifting. But it is also used for correction, re-direction, and re-adjusting our thoughts and attitudes. Bob shares very candidly about how God walked him and his family through struggles with aging parents.

His book is poignant, respectful, and insightful. It is also tough to put down!

Despite all the storms Bob and his family were experiencing, I love that he recognized the blessings that God incorporated into his experience. Bob has a great gift of music that he cultivates and shares with his family, his church family, and now our local senior community.

Every day is a gift from God! Enjoy your family and the time you have with them.

Thank you, Bob, for sharing your family's story.

Vaughn and Tamy Cook, friends from King Street Church